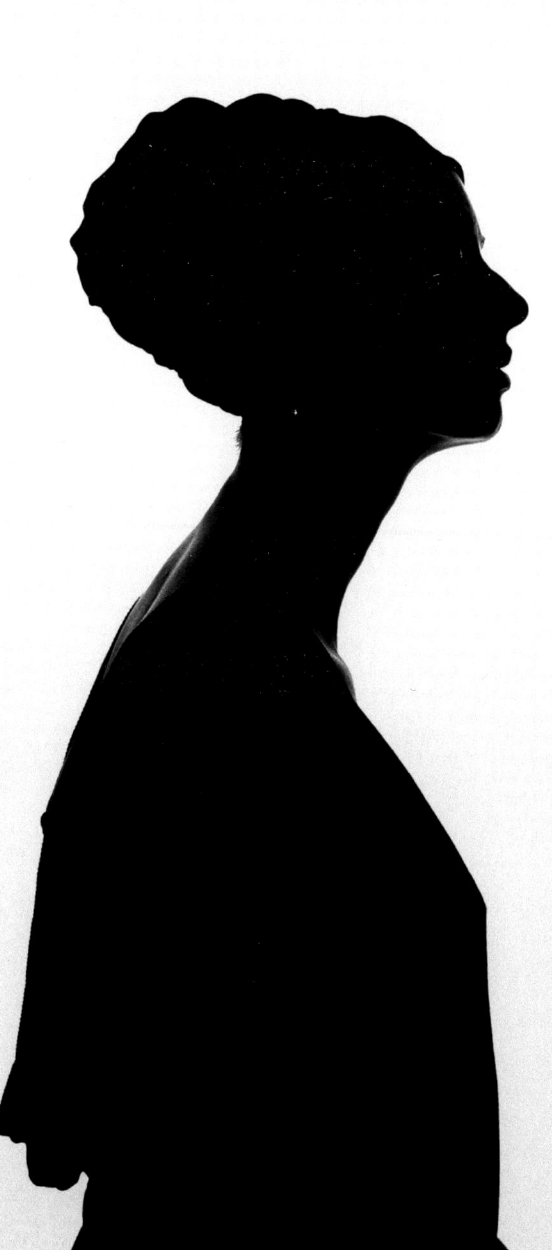

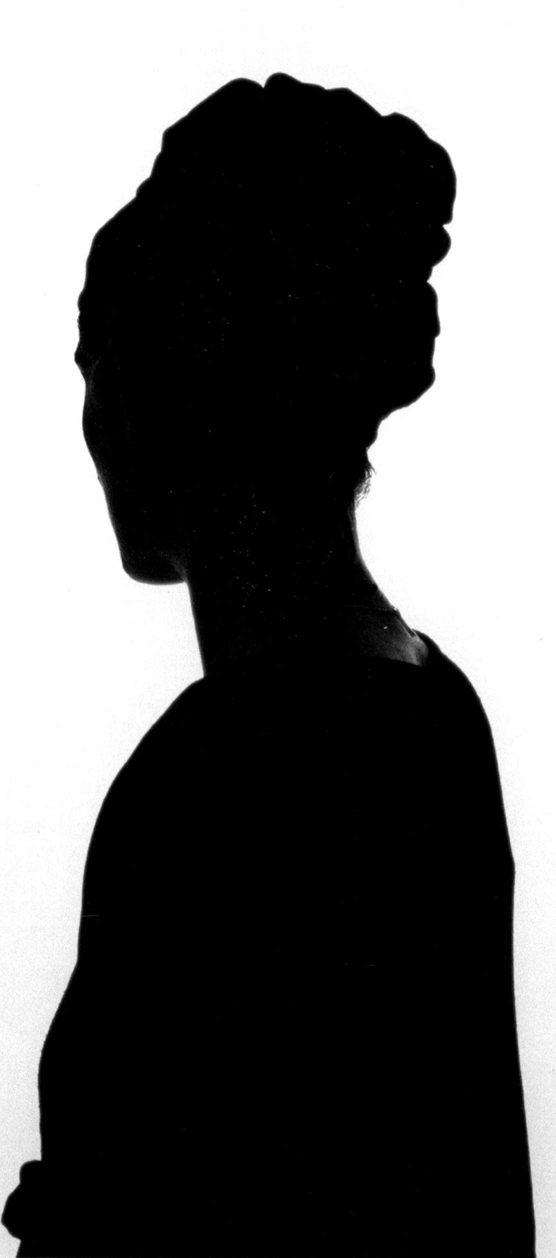

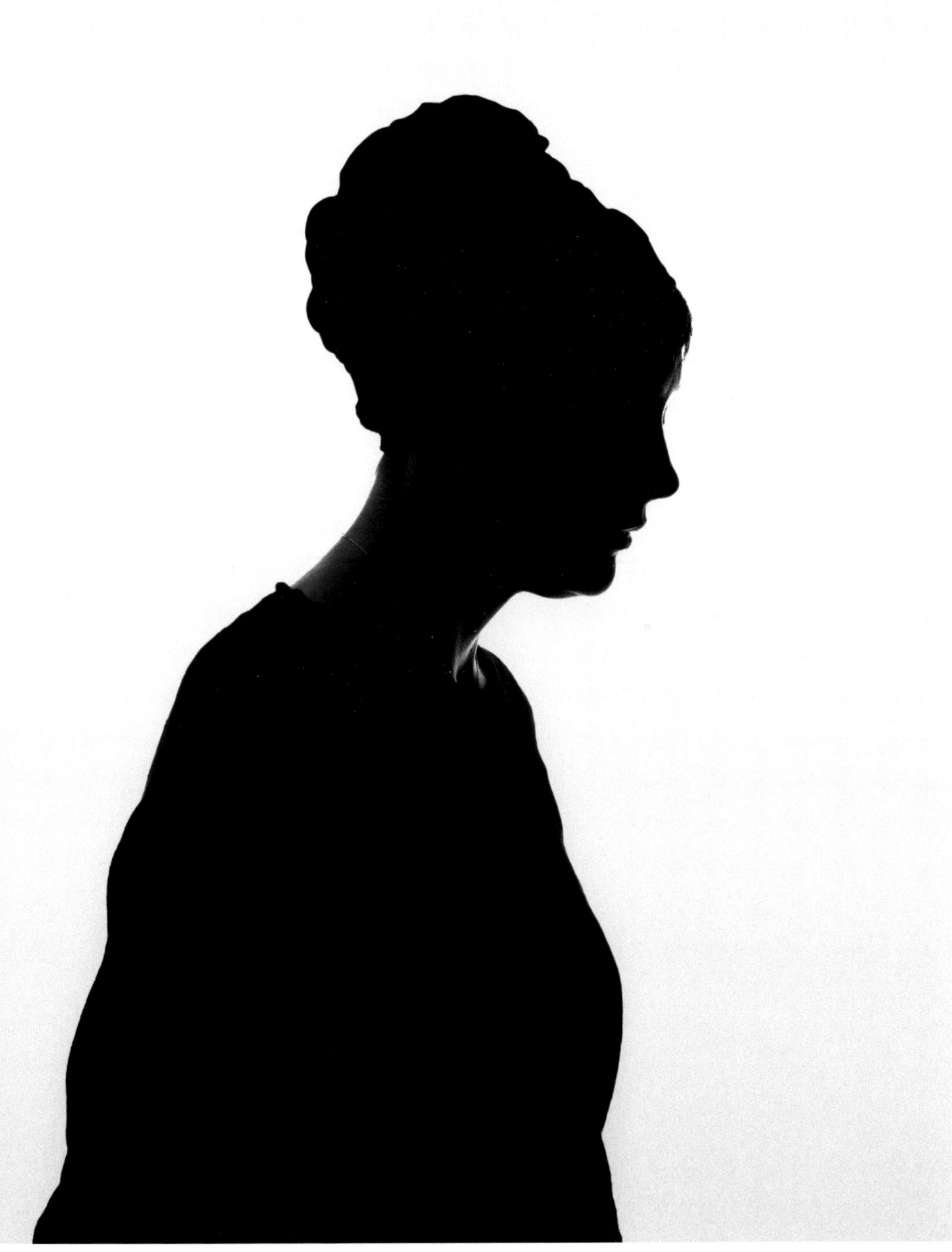

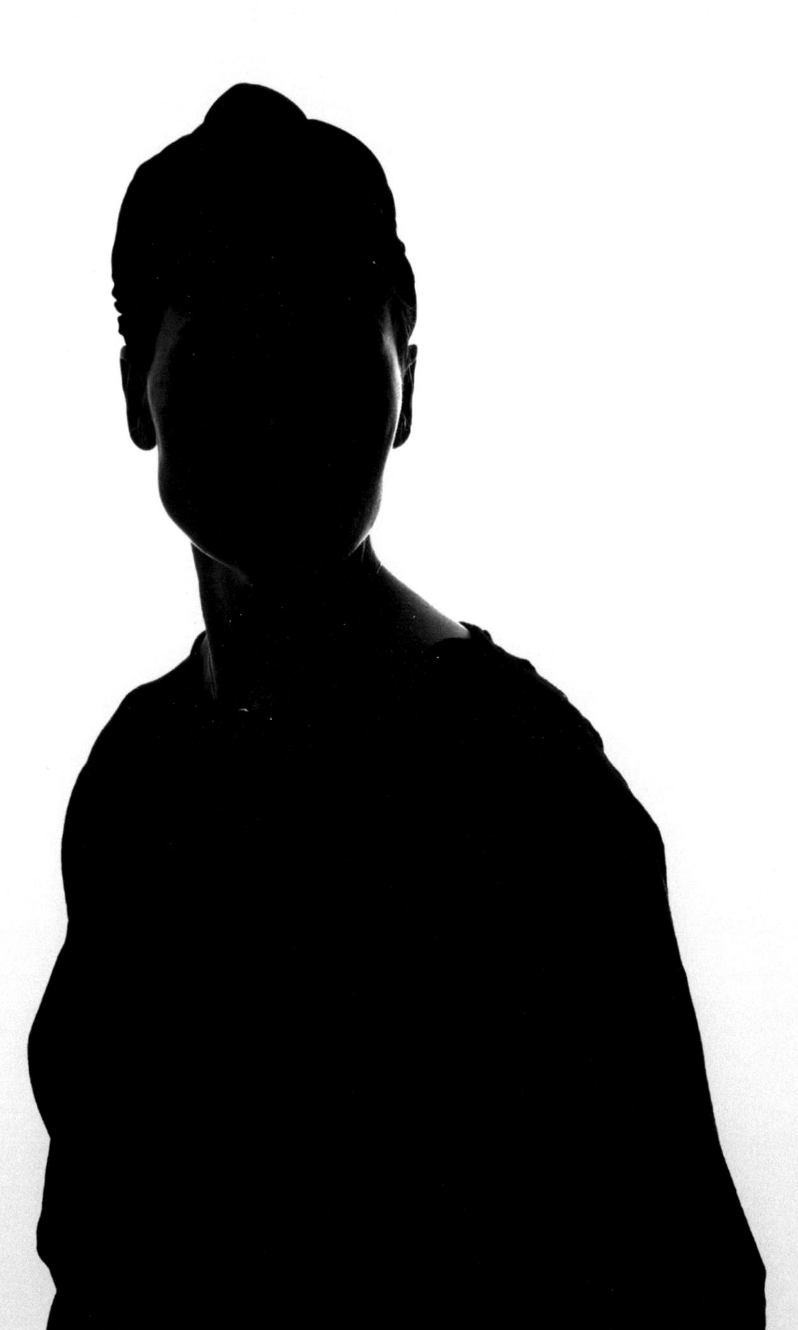

Lament

Lament

Bettina von Zwehl

Josh Cohen

with photographs by
Bettina von Zwehl

and

a short story and essay by
Josh Cohen

ART/BOOKS

Only

after

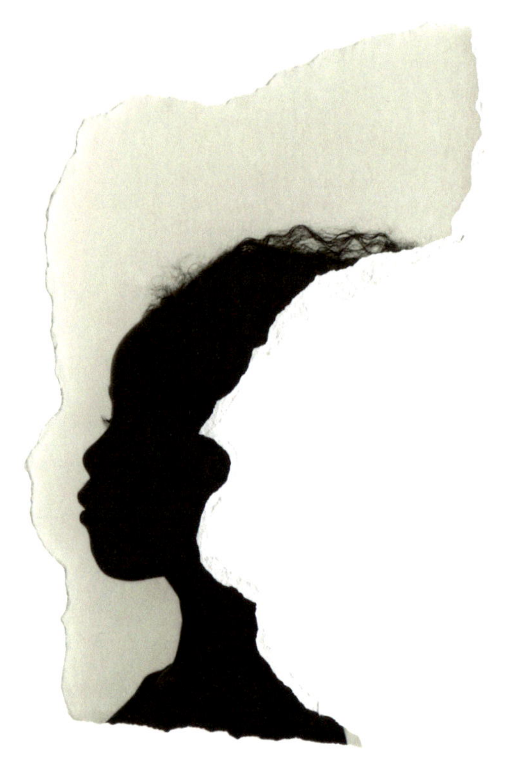

the

first photograph

came

did Wakeman

realize

how long he'd found
the faces of children
unbearable to look at.

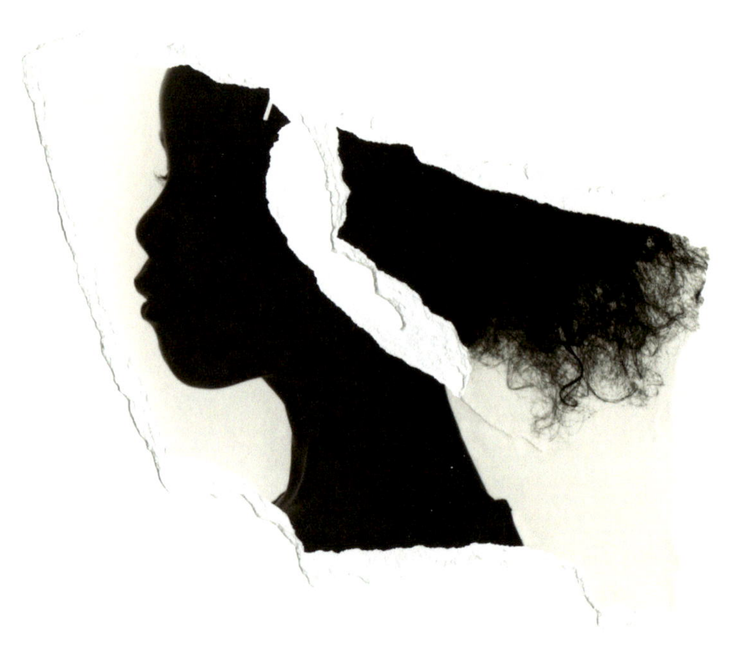

How, on the Tube, the merest hint of a small child opposite – a tiny nylon-padded body propped regally beside her fussing mother, snatches of infantile babble straining over the coach's clatter – would cause his gaze to avert itself sharply. He didn't know why, but neither had he thought much about it until now, as though the question were as unapproachable as the face itself.

It was a relief, then, to get off at his station and lose himself in the funereal shuffle to the exit, the short walk to the bank where he worked, the childless world in which he knew where he was, if nothing else.

But the photograph, its reverse side stamped and marked with his neatly biroed initials and address, was not to be so easily eluded. Slumped at the bottom of his short staircase for he knew not how long – a few seconds, an hour, a morning? – he stared near-catatonically at the darkling face, barely perceptible behind a curtain of shadow. Only the wet tear that slid slowly over the corner of his mouth tickled him into awareness. He wiped it, stared quizzically at the moist film spread over the pad of his finger, and left the house.

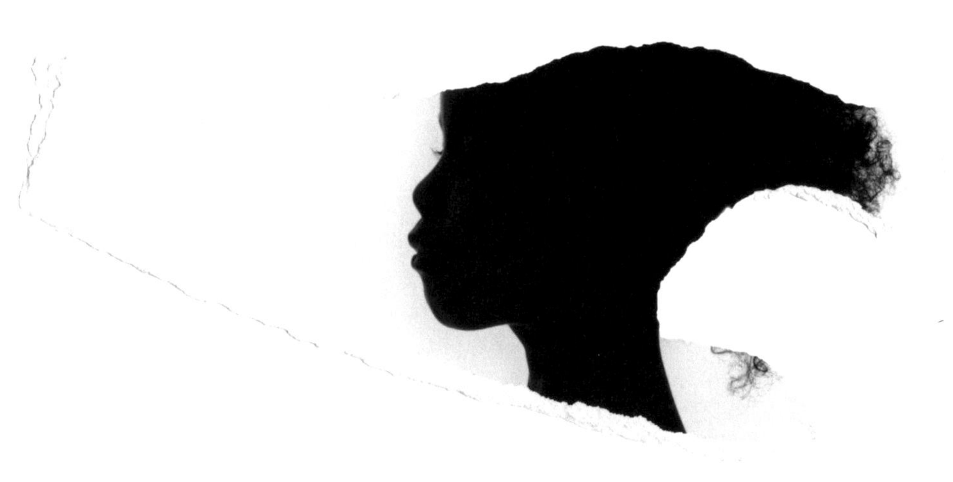

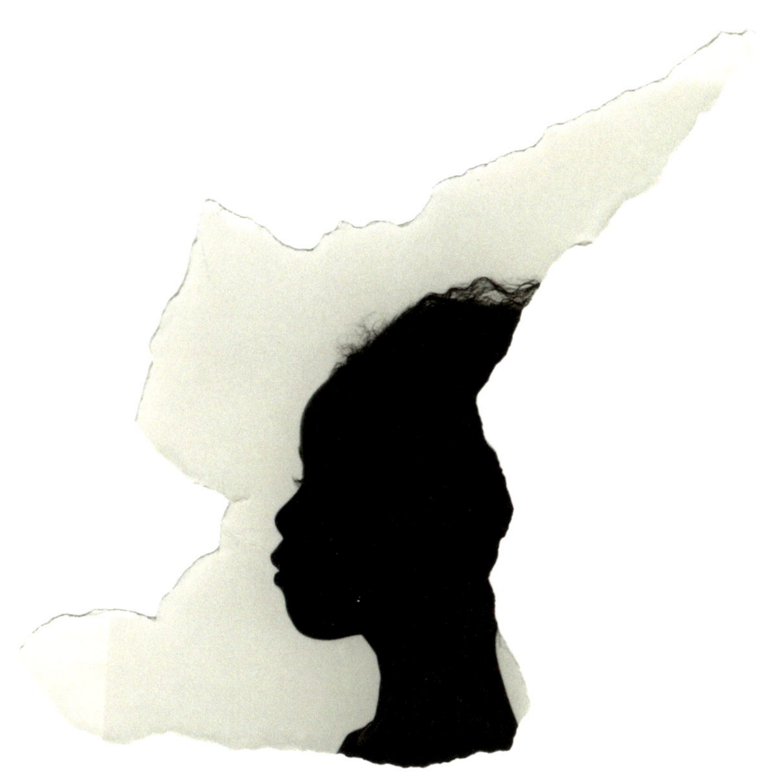

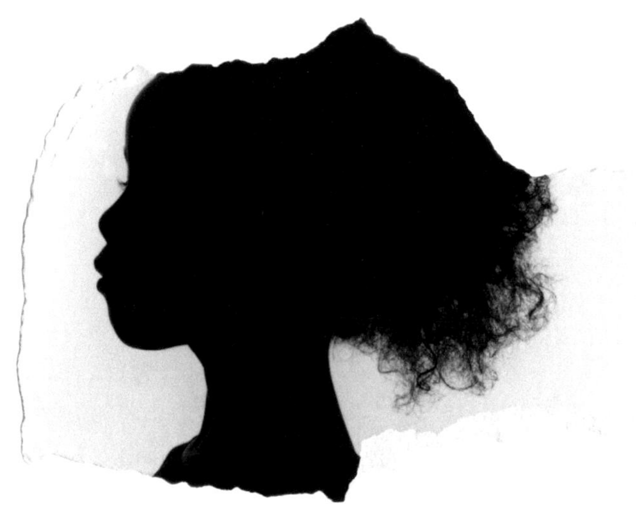

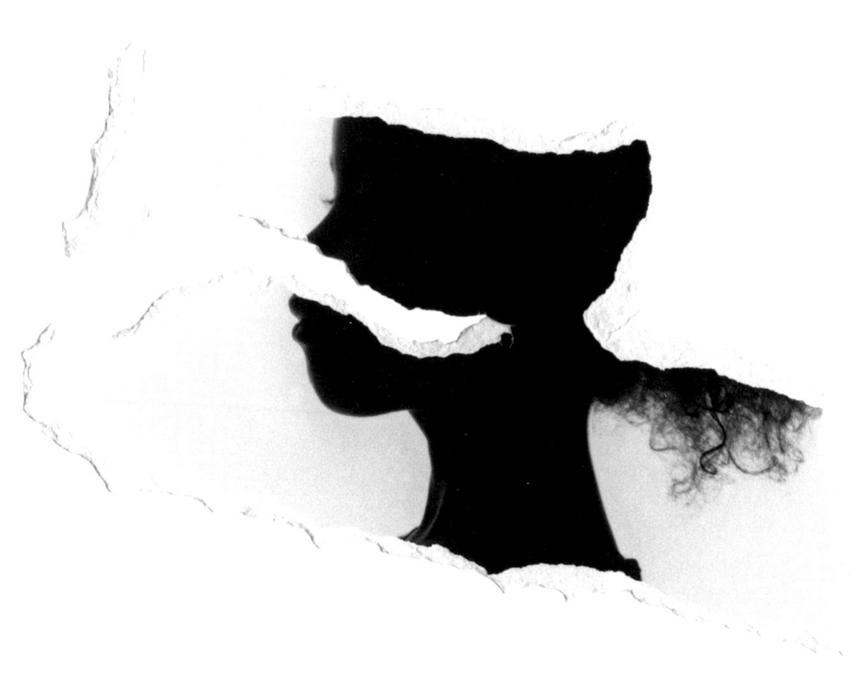

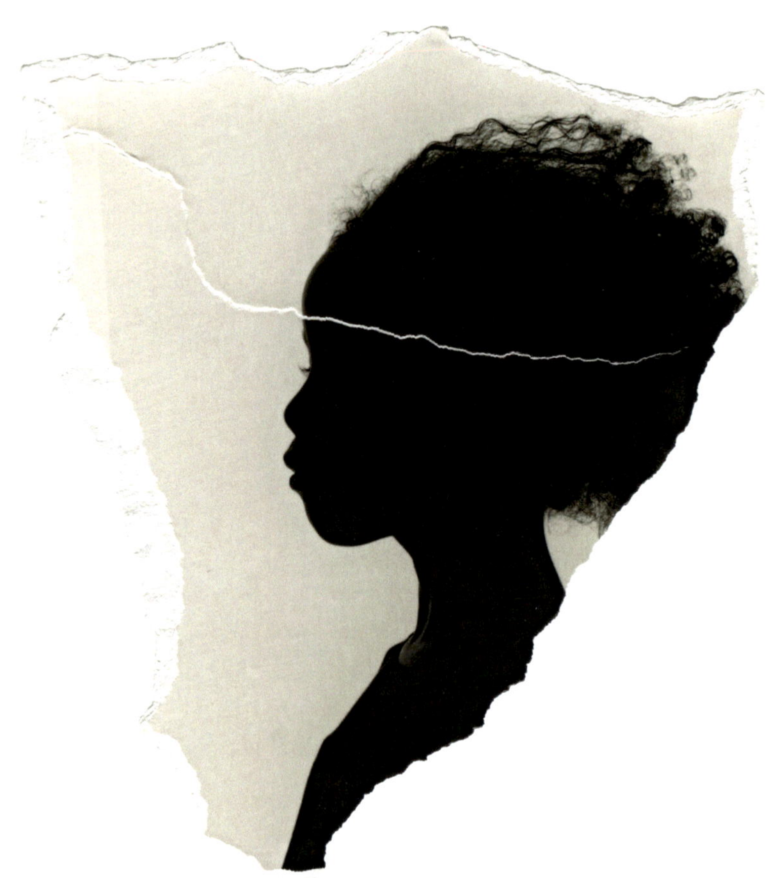

He might easily have missed it, thrown it out with the direct marketing and estate agents' circulars. Not a postcard, just a standard 6 × 4 print. A boy – six, seven? – staring into the middle distance, as though at some faraway light made more luminous by the darkness in which he is immersed. The outline and expression of his face seemed, impossibly, to resolve the longer and more deeply Wakeman stared into it, as though he had entered, and accustomed himself to, the very same darkness.

All he could see in the face at first was protest – against the camera, against the paper and retina on which his image would be imprinted. But the boy's furious wish not to be seen, not to submit to the loving or inquisitive or indifferent gaze of another, only stoked the compulsion to look at him regardless. This compulsion, he noted with surprise somewhere in the dark back of his mind, was at least as strong as the reflexive repulsion he felt in the presence of an actual child. He was riveted to the boy's defiance, his refusal to be looked at even as he was being looked at. He was faintly aware of some nagging and ridiculous fear that no sooner would he put the photo down than something would happen inside it.

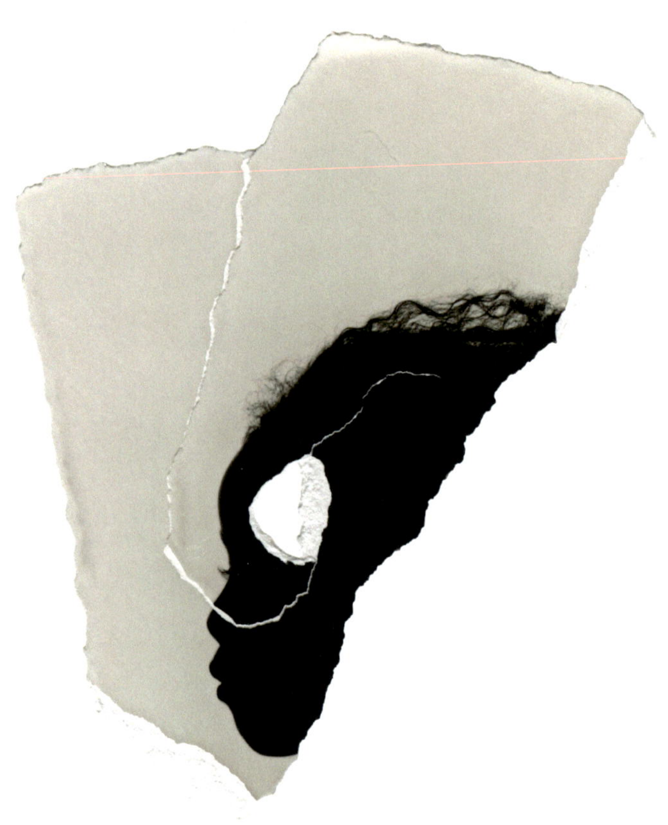

Walking to the station, he is grateful to the inexplicable tear that had jolted him out of his Cyclopic reverie – although he still feels cast in shadow, lost in quiet grief to the face that he has left lying on the bottommost stair.

INVITATION TO FREQUENT THE SHADOWS

A few months ago, during the brief interval between evening sessions, I tugged a little too tightly on the chord of my standard lamp. The bulb blew, upon which I realized I had forgotten to replenish the stock, leaving me to choose between conducting the next session in pitch darkness or under the harsh brightness of the ceiling lights. I made the only choice possible, though I still wonder if it was the right one.

The twilit illumination of the consulting room, along with the recumbent position on the couch and the quiet availability of the invisible analyst, is a way, as the jargon has it, of 'promoting regression'. It loosens the grip of the organized, logically consistent mental functioning of our daylight consciousness, enabling the analysand to regain contact with the nocturnal, associative logic of her psychic reality.

Although correct enough, this account misses something. It turns the setting of the analysis into a mere means, a set of preferred material conditions for the 'real' event of the patient's associations and the analyst's interpretations. But this floodlit session reminded me that there is no isolating the analytic exchange from the physical environment that makes it possible.

In spite of her reassuring insistence, in response to my explanation, that the bright light was fine, no problem, there was no mistaking the effect on her speech and my listening. The shadowy light of a consulting room suspends the analytic pair between the obscurity of dream life and the clarity of waking life; if it is banished, their words and gestures lose all but their most explicit sense. As she began talking about an incident at work, her voice assumed the impersonal tone of a courtroom witness: 'He seemed angry

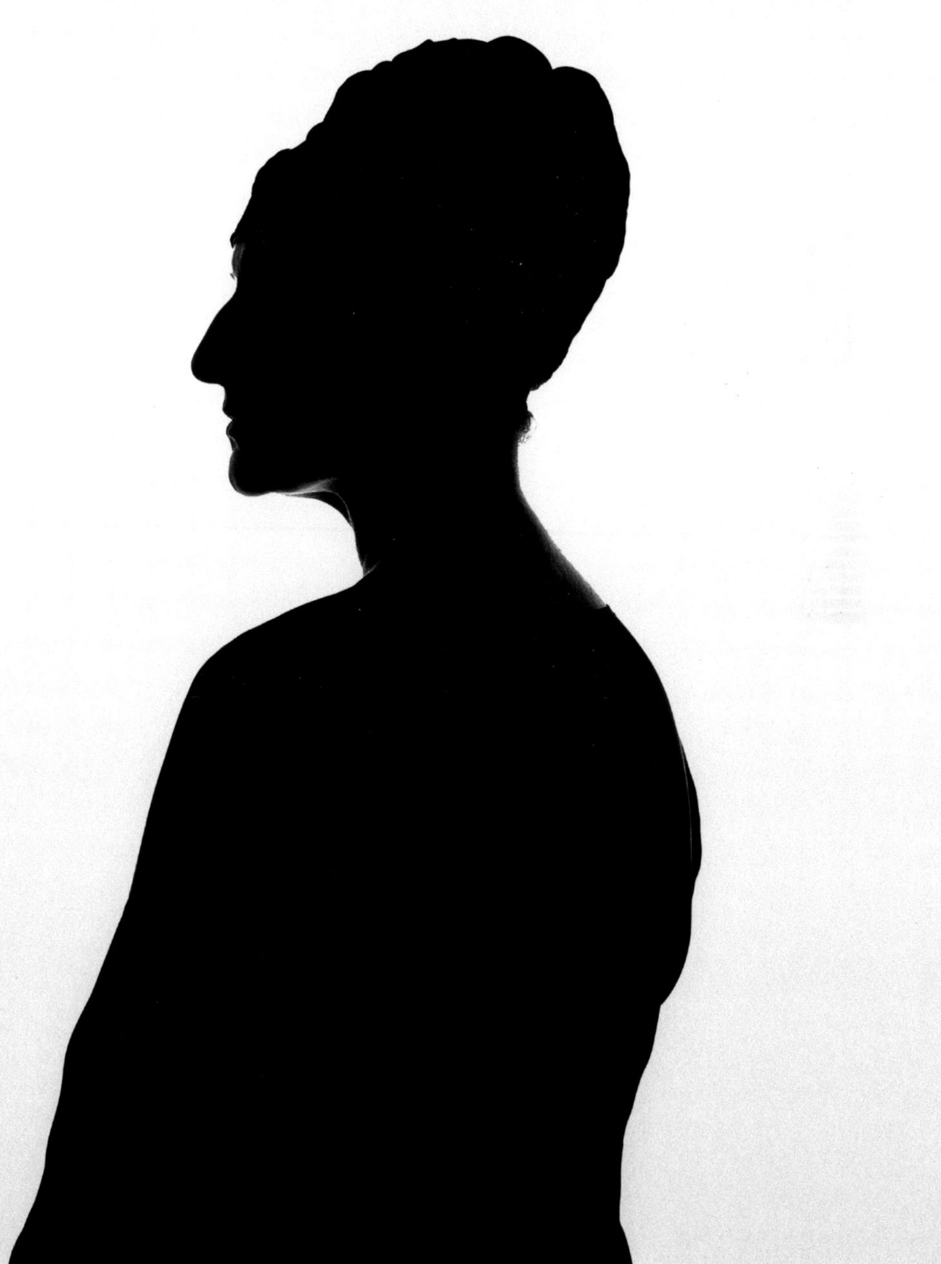

because I hadn't invoiced the client, but I told him that I'd not been asked.' In any case, it was only at such a constricted frequency that I could hear her, as though the light had bleached out all the ornate shadings of her words. I listened to the story she related as though all that she had wanted to tell me was what had happened.

Sensing the awkwardness, I wondered aloud if the brightness of the room were bothering her more than she wanted to say. Humming agreement, she quickly fell into a long silence. That silence, it struck me, was a kind of surrogate shadowy space into which her unconscious could creep back in, even if only as an absence. The shadows had been eradicated, discernible only in our silent, wishful longing for their return, as well as, I suspected, in her emerging, still unvoiced anger with me for their loss that evening.

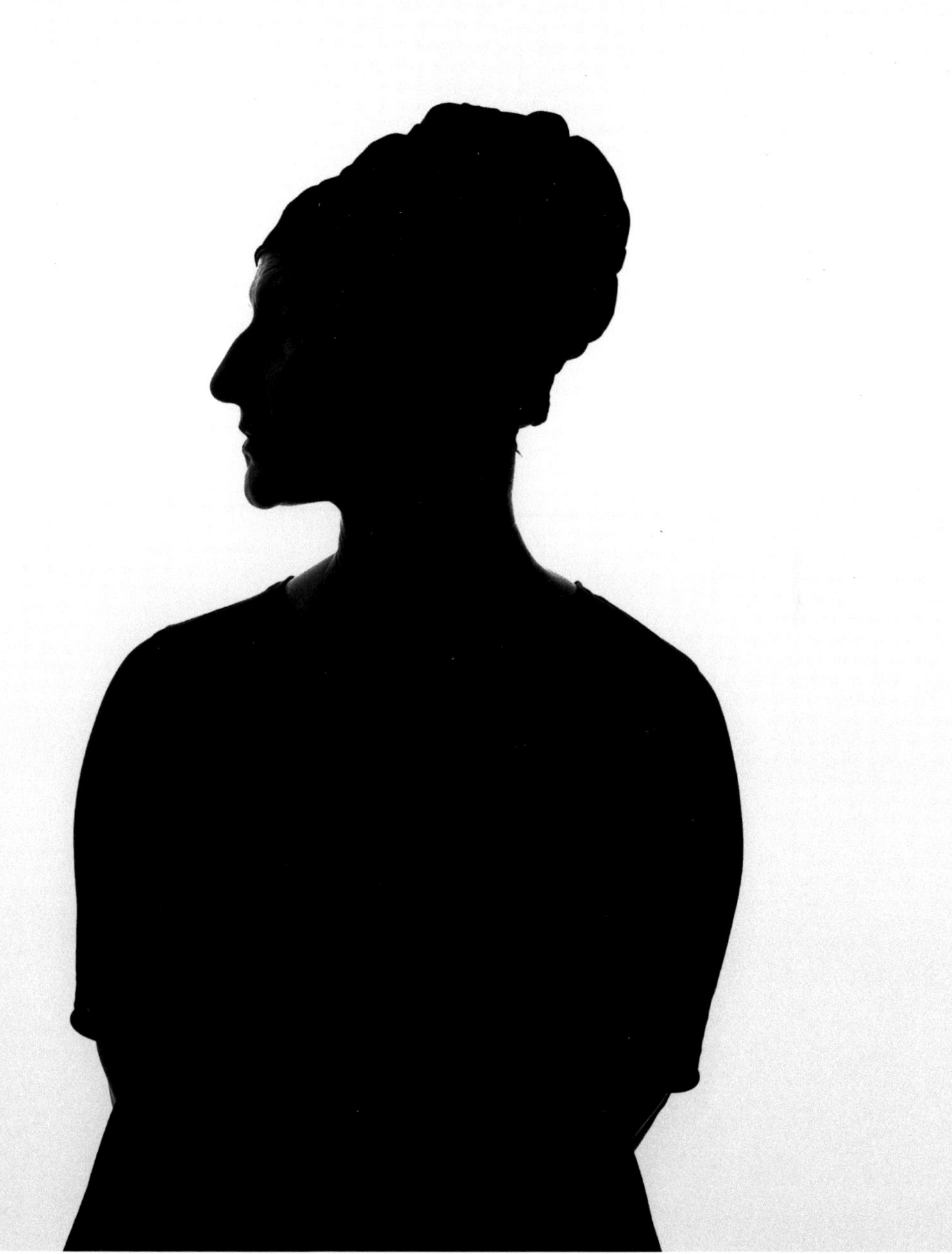

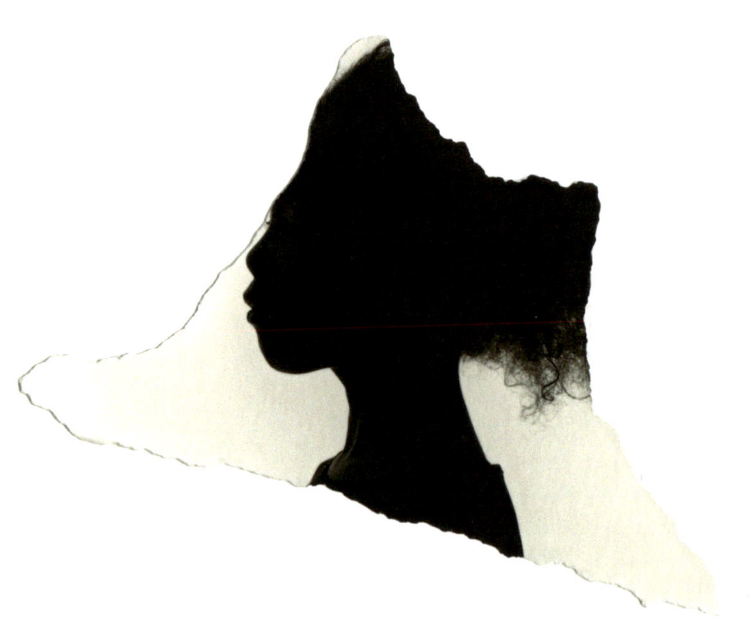

Wakeman knew to expect more, feeling no surprise as another one tumbled onto the hallway carpet the next day, oddly exposed amid the scattering of discrete buff and white envelopes.

He didn't ask himself who might have sent it – neither the ones already arrived, nor those yet to come. He was enough of this world to see that someone else in his shoes would by now be burning with furious curiosity, fear and rage, and that this reaction was the natural one to have, that he might be expected to feel some sense of threat, even violation, to respond by plunging himself actively into the discovery of the who and the why of these photos. He saw the logic of such a response, but couldn't make it his own.

Was this Wakeman's child? He could not take the question seriously, but nor could he help letting his mind's eye wander over the assorted desultory couplings of years past. On the Tube home, he shut his eyes, let his head sway with the carriage and saw himself propped tightly on his wrists, raised over the torso of one or other woman, pretty or plain, his arms opening a chasm between their skins.

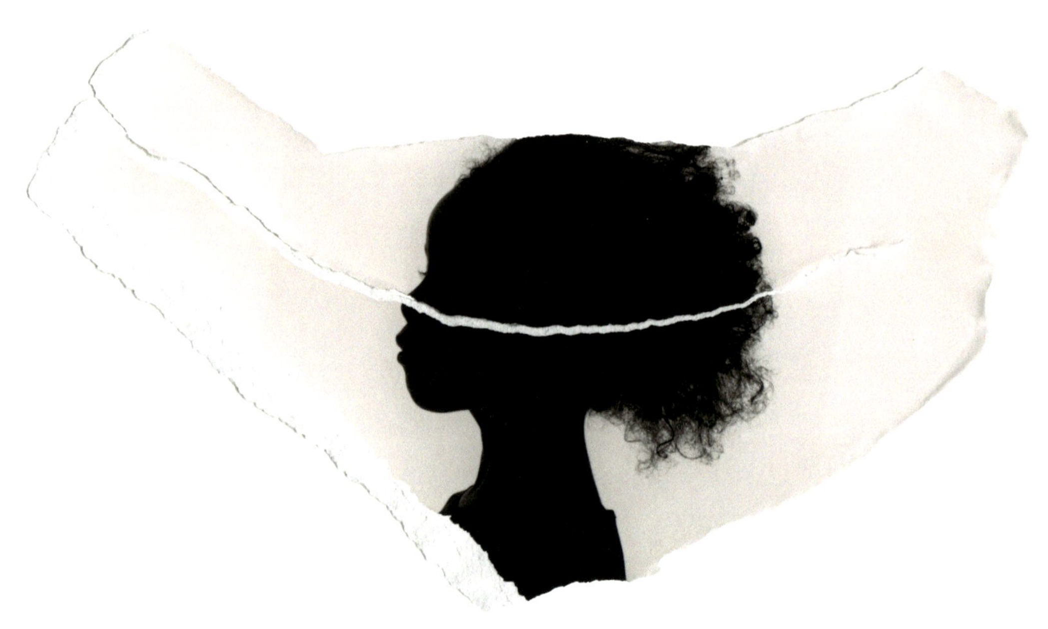

He found it oddly consoling to imagine a link between the daily apparition on his hallway floor and these episodes of loveless need, as though the sudden rip in the fabric of his ordered life could be sewn up with the seamlessness of bad television. If only he could believe that this would all play out as some tired dramatic cliché, perhaps he would not feel the expanding hole burning in his gut with every flap of his letterbox. 'You see,' a woman's muffled voice might say through the receiver, 'it was just that night, and I knew I had no right to ask anything of you. And so I couldn't bring myself to tell you, but now, you see, I'm ill, very ill, and I think it's time you knew.'

But he was certain no stories could make sense of the arrival of these photos. The feeling struck him again and again that the boy couldn't be accounted for, didn't want to be railroaded into showing or telling anything. He would guess his age as sometimes seven, sometimes five, but never younger, as though his earliest life belonged to some impossible prehistoric epoch from which all cameras and all eyes had been banned, as though he had come into the world as this fully formed child.

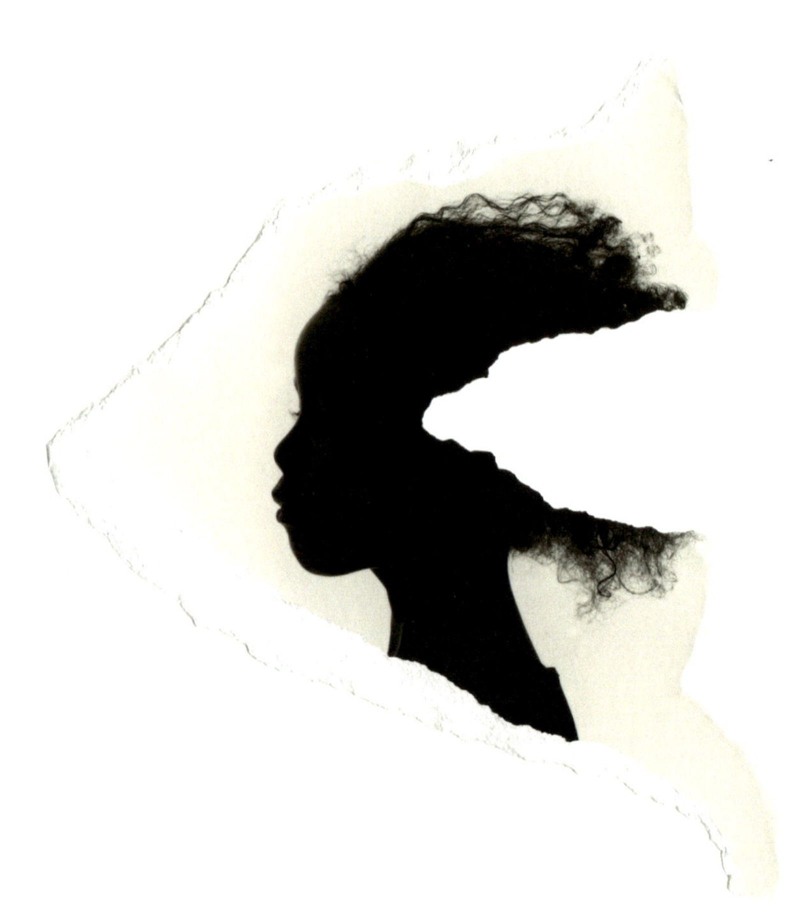

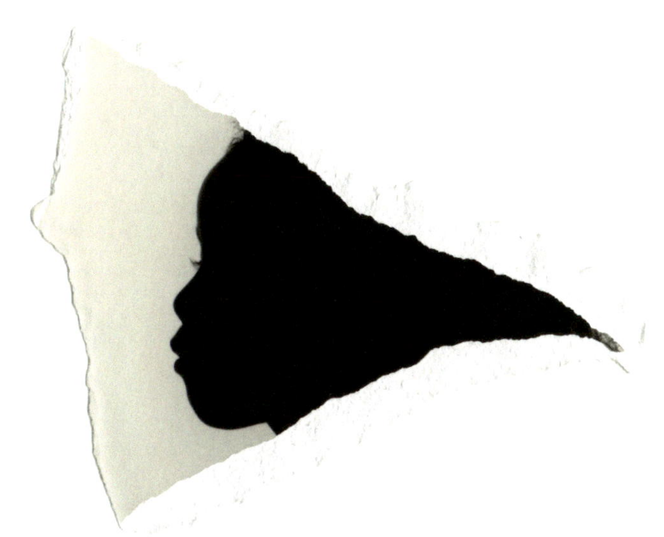

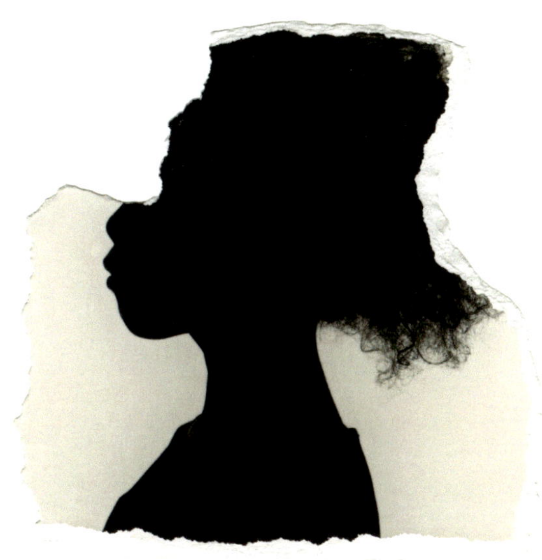

The shutter button clicks, the aperture opens, light reaches and captures the object. We call this sequence, today so intricately woven into the grammar and rhythm of our everyday perception, an *exposure*. An ambiguous term, signalling the active and passive poles of the same experience, the word unites the radically disparate positions of exposer and exposed, as though there were a secret complicity between the two, some point where they shade into one another.

More than eighty years ago, novelist Junichirō Tanizaki lamented the ceiling lights that flooded the rooms of the 'most recent Western-style buildings' then mushrooming all over Japan, which served 'no function but to eradicate every trace of shadow'. No longer contained within the discretion of four walls, those ceiling lights are now the very element of our daily existence. The proliferation of our digital doubles across social media, location services, self-tracking apps and CCTV place us in a state of permanent luminosity and transparency.

This flood of light contracts the spaces in which shadows can abide. Birth, sex and grief, the life cycle's deepest intimacies, are daily exposed as though only their permanent broadcast could confer meaning and significance upon them. The virtual world invites us to share the intricate data of our bodily and neuro-chemical lives, to record and upload our every waking moment. Under these conditions of tacitly coerced self-disclosure, the distinction between exposer and exposed inexorably dissolves; once shadowless light becomes the medium of life, and experience acquires meaning, even existence, only insofar as it is visible, the question whether we are the active agents or passive victims of our own exposure loses all sense. Exposure is the condition in which we no longer know the difference.

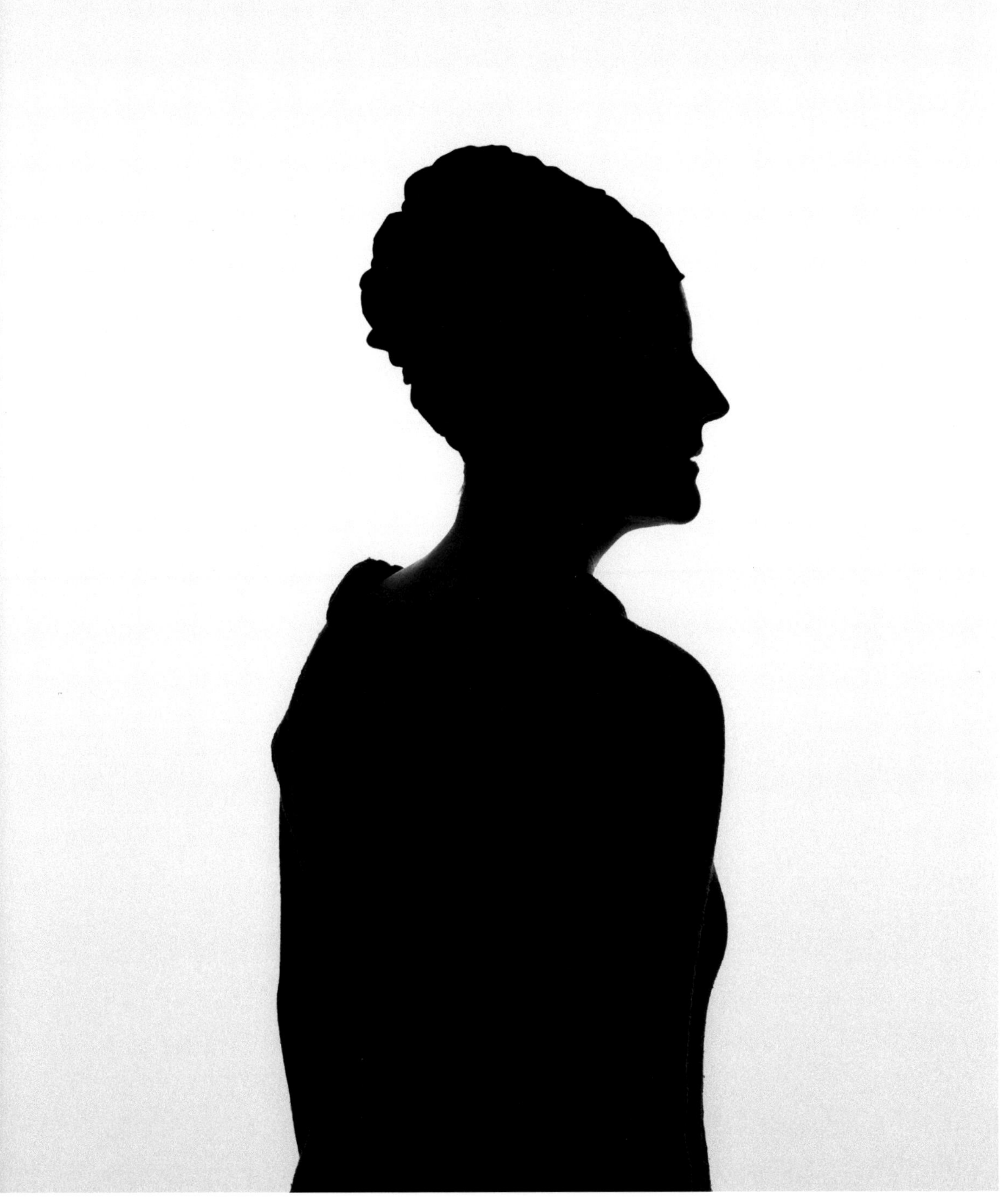

Each

day

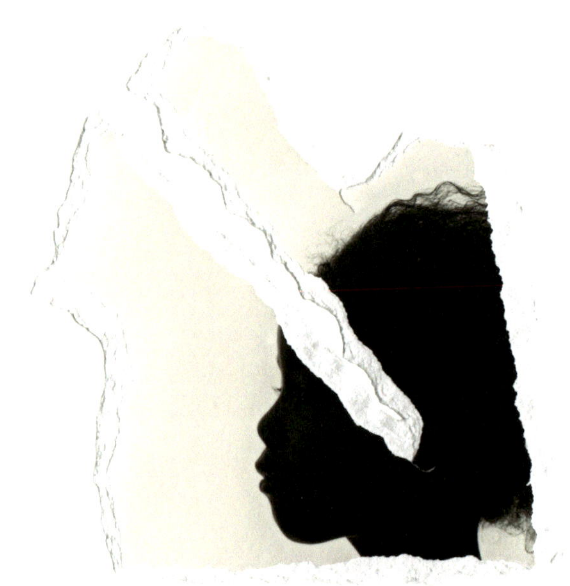

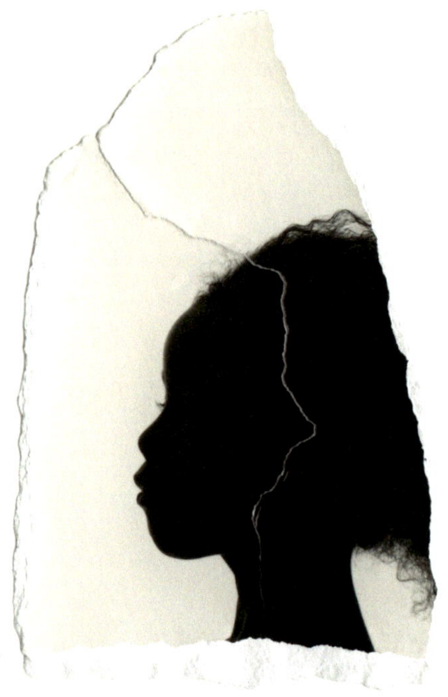

the

same photograph

in

different

iterations:

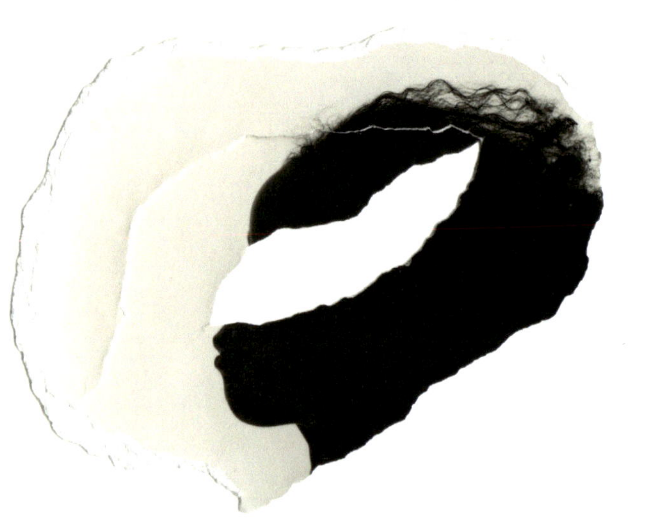

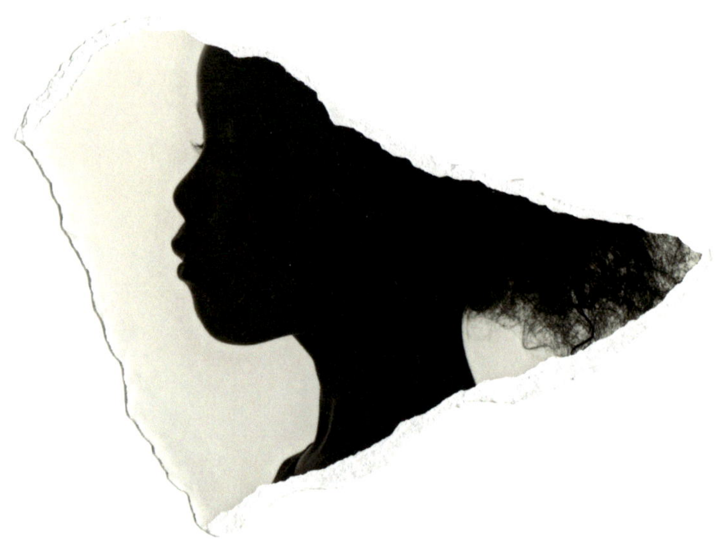

the face shrouded in shadow or flooded by brightness, sometimes spilling over the edges of the paper, sometimes a barely discernible spot at its centre. He strained to make out its expression, the tiny but decisive contortions of its features, one day seeing only simmering contempt in the glint of the boy's wide eyes; the next, some obscure intimation of perfect joy; yet another, an indelible sadness.

Wakeman had known straight away, without needing to say it to himself, that in asking who the child was he would only be asking who he was himself. On the wall to his side, his profile hovered over the base of the mirror's frame. He imagined his reflected face turning and looking at its double, rooted to the bottom stair, boring his eyes into the images with such blind zeal, as though if he stayed with them long enough, letting the half-hours slip imperceptibly away, they would yield up the secret that would free him from them once and for all.

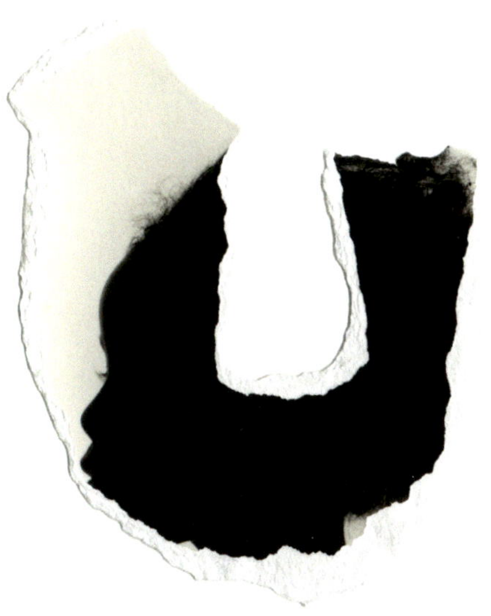

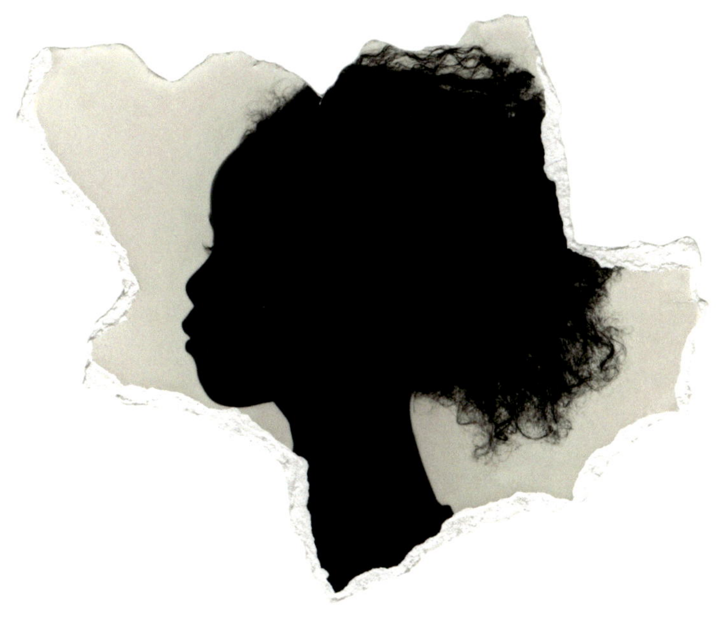

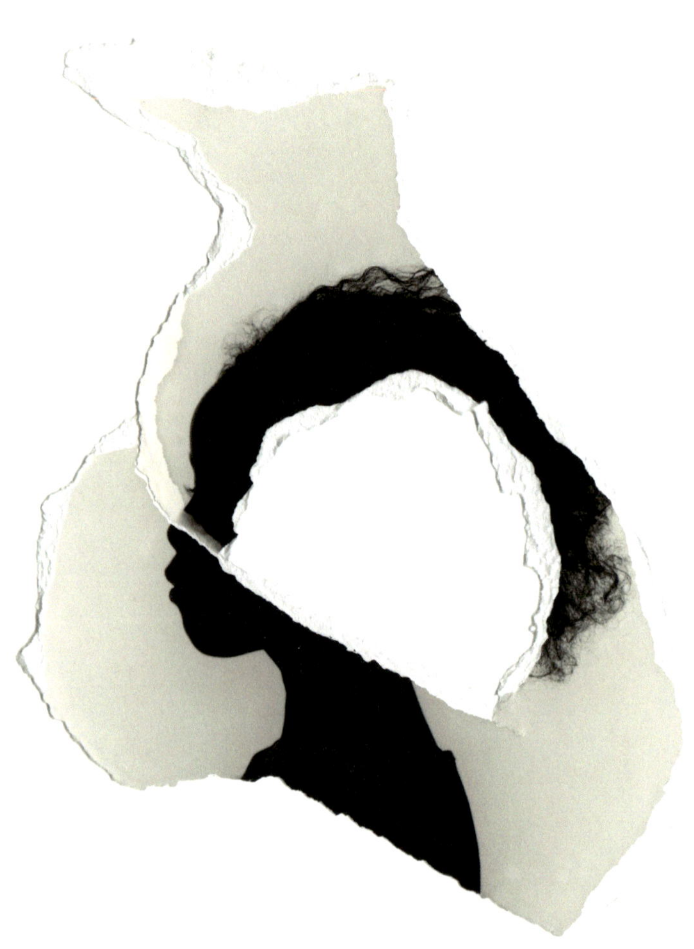

But each day the secret seemed to recede further and deeper behind the image, until he wanted to plunge his whole hand into its invisible insides. He couldn't fathom what these images wanted of him, him for whom every child was a locked room whose key had long since been lost. The face, irradiated with passion, brimming with playfulness, belonged to a world he knew nothing about.

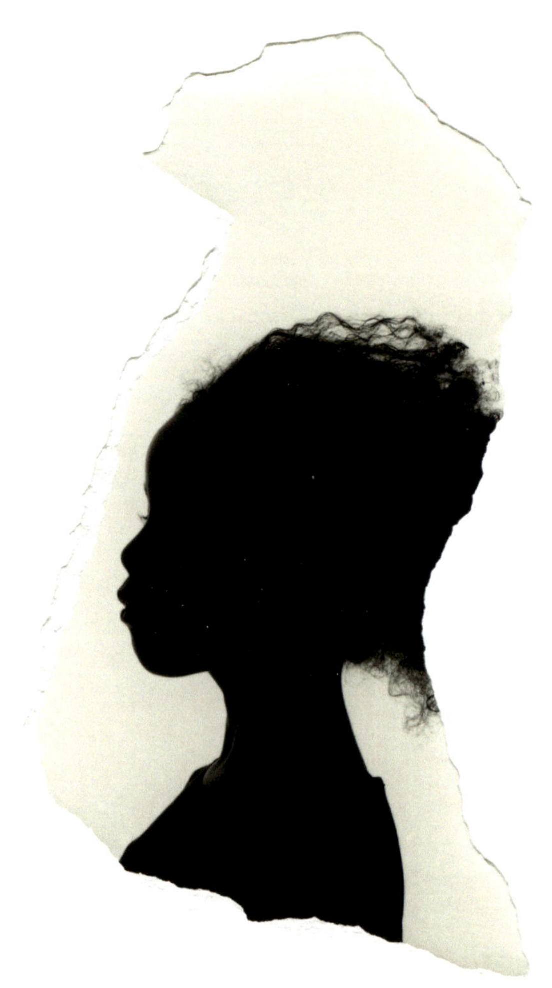

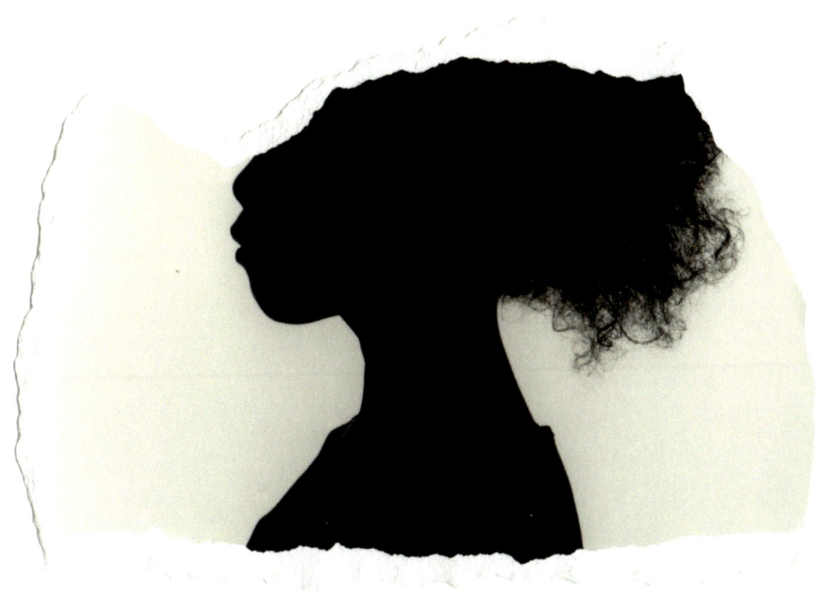

Tanizaki's ceiling lights and their drive to eliminate the shadows could be said to have their origin in Plato's cave, whose shadows have long been our preferred synonym for error, illusion and untruth. The mythic denizens of the grim chamber, shackled from birth at the legs and neck, and so prevented from turning their heads, can see only what is directly before them. Light emanates from a fire behind them, in front of which is a small wall, 'like the screen at puppet shows between the operators and their audiences'. Behind the screen, people carry along a range of artefacts – human and animal figures carved of stone and wood, whose shadows are projected onto the wall of the cave.

Never having learned otherwise, the cave-dwellers take 'the shadows of the artefacts' for 'the whole truth' (*aletheia* – literally, 'the unconcealed'). When one of them is released from his shackles and stumbles towards the fire, he is dazzled by its 'flickering brightness'. In the face of the blinding light, he retreats back to the shadows; told that the objects passing before the fire are more real than the projections on the cave wall, he clings tenaciously to his prior illusions, trusting the relative clarity of the shadow play over the blur of real objects.

Those prisoners, Socrates tells Glaucon, 'are very much like us'. Reared in ignorance, we too are caught in an illusory trap, condemned to confuse truth with its insubstantial shadows. Later in *The Republic*, the most pernicious manifestation of this confusion will turn out to be our love of art, which impels us wilfully to turn our minds from truth to simulacra, from real things to their shadowy doubles.

And so Plato is said to inaugurate the war of light against shadow. But is this to understand him too quickly?

If the prisoners of the cave are 'very much like us', then their existence in the cave describes more than a provisional and degraded state of ignorance and privation. It portrays immersion in the shadows as the very condition of being human. In his commentary on the cave allegory, Martin Heidegger writes that 'being human ... means ... to stand within the *hidden*, to be

And

surrounded by the hidden'. The hidden is not, in other words, some external impediment to truth whose removal would render it to us whole and transparent. It is on the contrary an integral dimension of truth. Distilling the essence of the allegory, Heidegger writes that 'concealment belongs *essentially* to unhiddenness [that is, to truth], *like the valley belongs to the mountain*.' Or: 'Untruth *belongs* to the essence of truth.'

There is much more than a contest of interpretations at stake in how we understand the cave allegory. To read Plato as seeking the eradication of shadow from the world is to assume an imperative to abolish obscurity and hiddenness. This would make the paparazzo a model Platonist. Doesn't his unsparing drive to penetrate all those doors and walls that separate us from the secrets of others, his conquest of the distance between us and those others by means of telephoto lenses or hacking devices, make him a frontline warrior in the war on shadows? And insofar as he dedicates himself unsparingly to capture by light, to exposure, does he not embody the essential spirit of photography?

If Heidegger is right, on the other hand, the paparazzo is a very careless reader of Plato indeed, for in seeking to shine light into every corner of the hidden, he loses sight of the hidden itself as a necessary and irreducible dimension of reality. In dismissing privacy, in his testimony to the Leveson Inquiry, as necessary only 'for paedos', the tabloid journalist Paul McMullan was denying shadow any right to a place in the world.

Can we imagine a photography that would protect, rather than banish, the hiddenness of the object?

still

they came,

until he found himself praying for them to stop even as he rushed to retrieve them from the pile of unopened mail onto which they now dropped. Each swept in from some distant shore three thousand miles or three streets away, from two decades or two days ago.

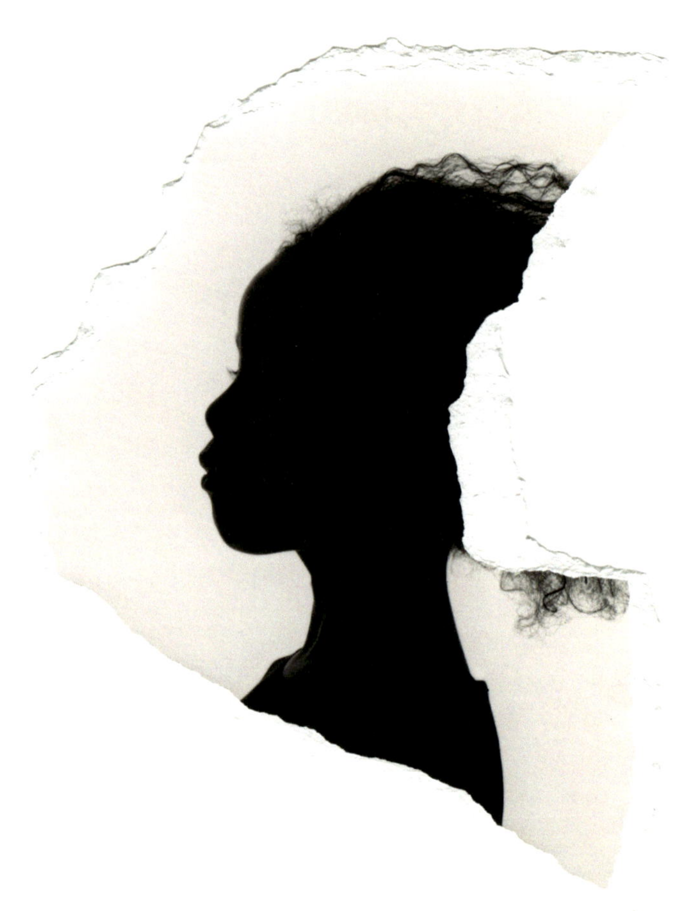

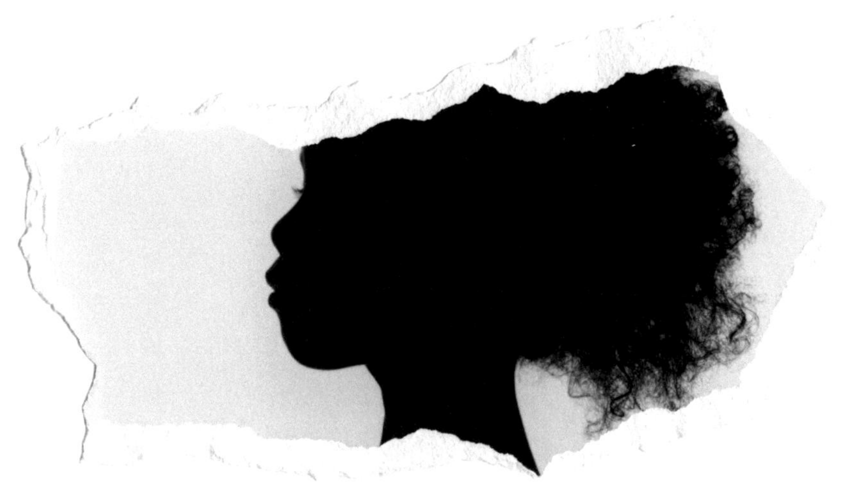

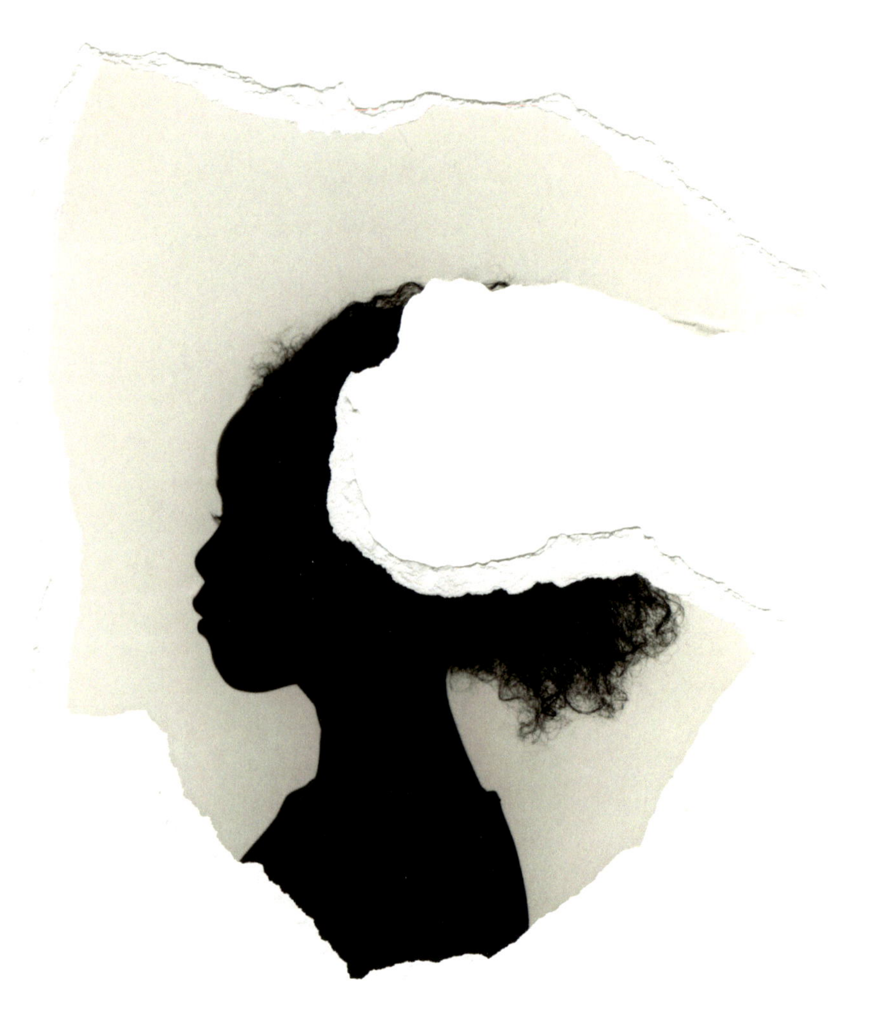

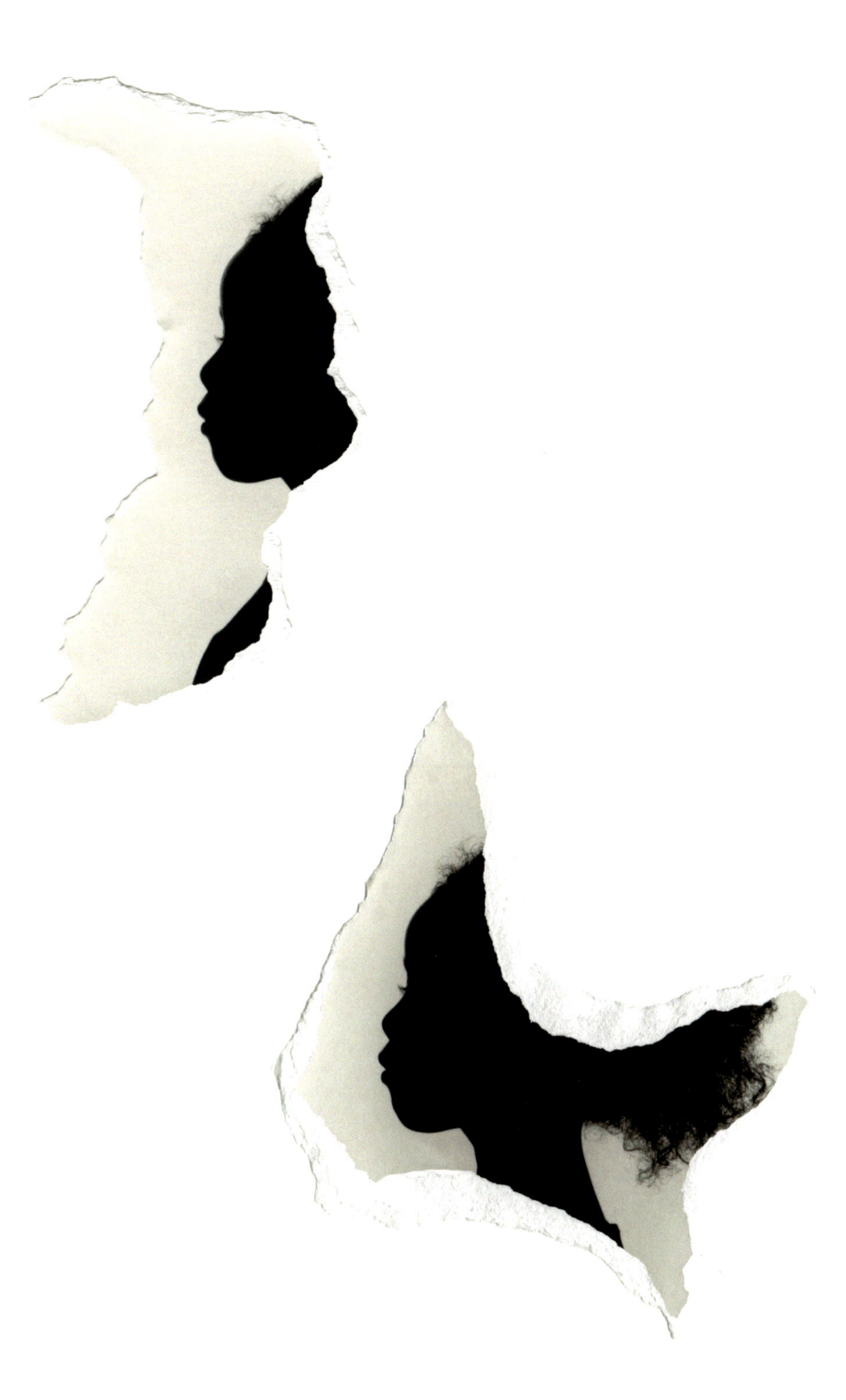

Years of early arrivals at the bank had given way within days to mere punctuality, and within weeks to casual lateness. His meticulousness gave way to a distracted competence, as his admired and resented dedication fell slowly but decisively away. He made minor mathematical errors, grimaced irritably, forgot a client meeting, his pristine immaculacy gathering smudges of ordinary humanity.

He said nothing about it to anyone. What was he going to say, and to whom? There was no one who would reward his confidence with anything other than a barrage of stupid questions and lurid speculations, who would not smugly enjoy the spectacle of his aloof pride cracking open. He didn't yet know what his questions were, but he was certain they would not be the same as any would-be confidant's.

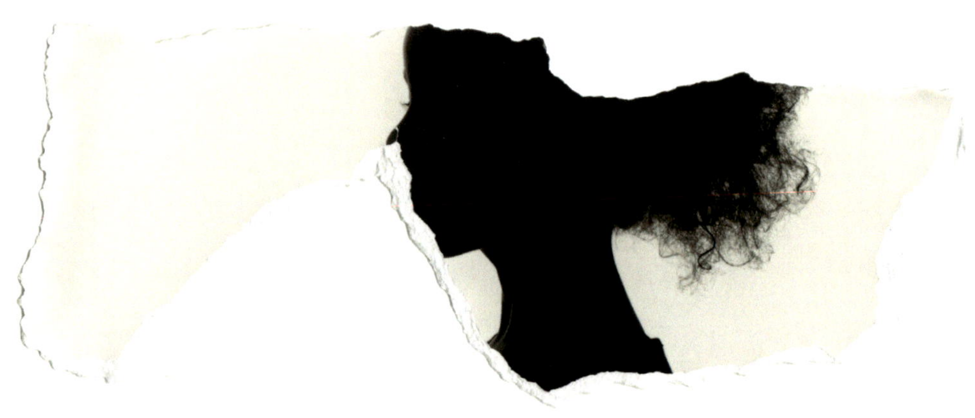

However reliably they arrived, he never ceased to feel the same thrill of pain each time.

The image may have been the same,

but

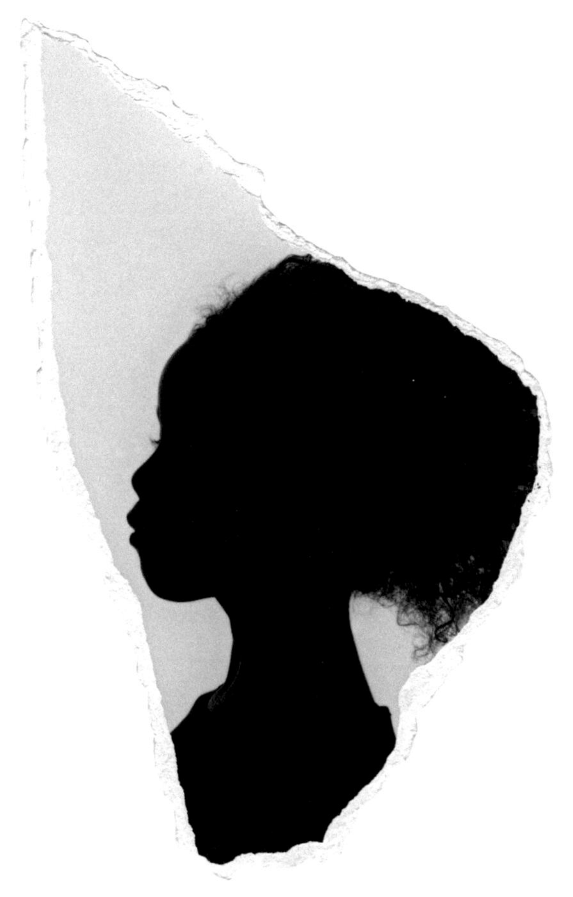

each print renewed the shock with
some near-imperceptible adjustment
in brightness or focus or distance.

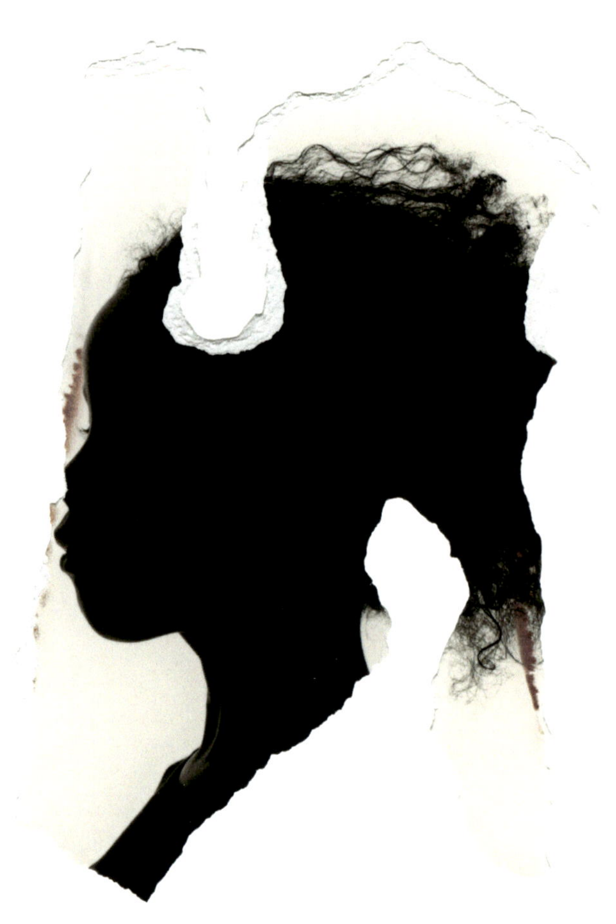

Before the advent of the ceiling lights, Tanizaki suggests, Japanese interiors manifested a relationship of intimacy, rather than enmity, between light and dark. The pleasure of Japanese architecture and decorative arts lay in their cultivation of a certain indistinctness, a dreamy blurring of the edges between inside and outside, one thing and the next. Where the soup in a modern ceramic bowl is revealed in 'every nuance of its substance and colour', the Japanese lacquerware bowl renders itself barely distinguishable from the liquid within: 'There is a beauty in that moment between removing the lid and lifting the bowl to the mouth when one gazes at the still, silent liquid in the dark depths of the bowl, its colour hardly differing from that of the bowl itself.'

With Japan's Westernization, this ambiguous beauty was increasingly lost to the rule of clarity and differentiation. It is instructive to set Tanizaki's image of the dark soup's merger with the bowl alongside the food photography that so compulsively punctuates today's Sunday supplements, TV ads and Instagram feeds, in which the dishes are arranged and lit so as to achieve an intense, granular vividness. Not for nothing is this photographic sub-genre known as 'food porn', and not for nothing do its practitioners play so archly on the luxuriant unctuousness glistening from the page. Like porn, food photography exposes us to our own voracious desires at least as much as to the sensual textures of the food, catching us, as it were, in the shaming act of wanting something. In contrast to Tanizaki's scene, in which the anticipated flavour of the soup – and by implication our desire for it – is enhanced by the obscure play of shadows, neither the object nor the viewer of the contemporary food photograph is afforded the discretion of a hiding place. The private pleasures of eating must be dragged into the light.

In this dazzling culture, Tanizaki suggests, art and literature provide us with a last outpost of shadowy ambiguity: 'In the mansion called literature, I would have the eaves deep and the walls dark, I would push back into the shadows the things that come forward too clearly.'

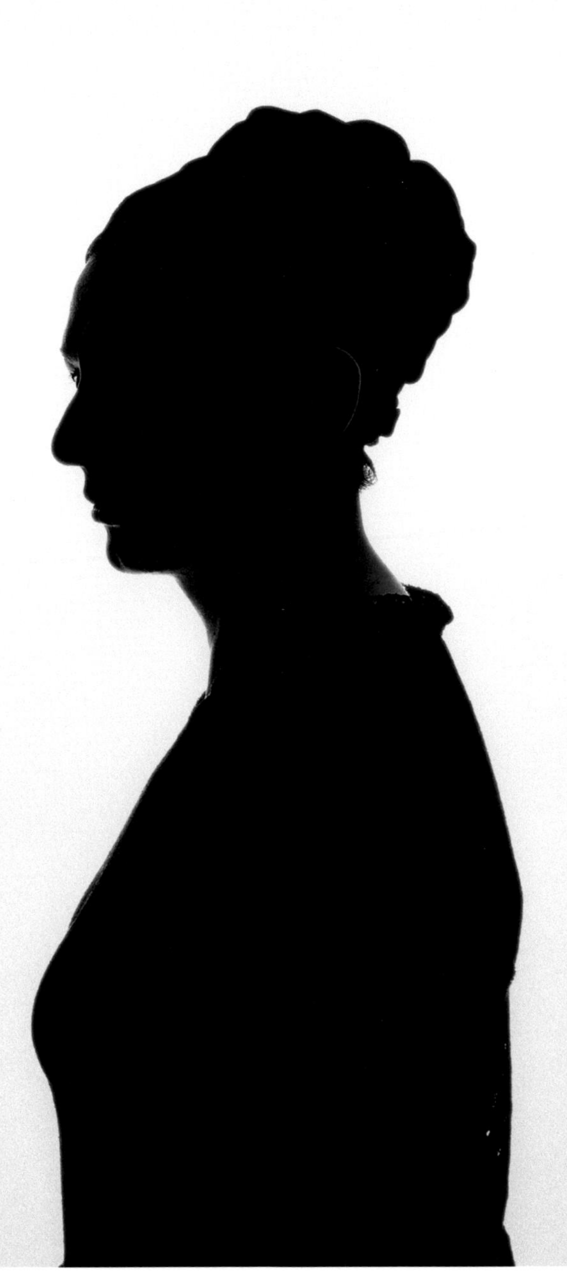

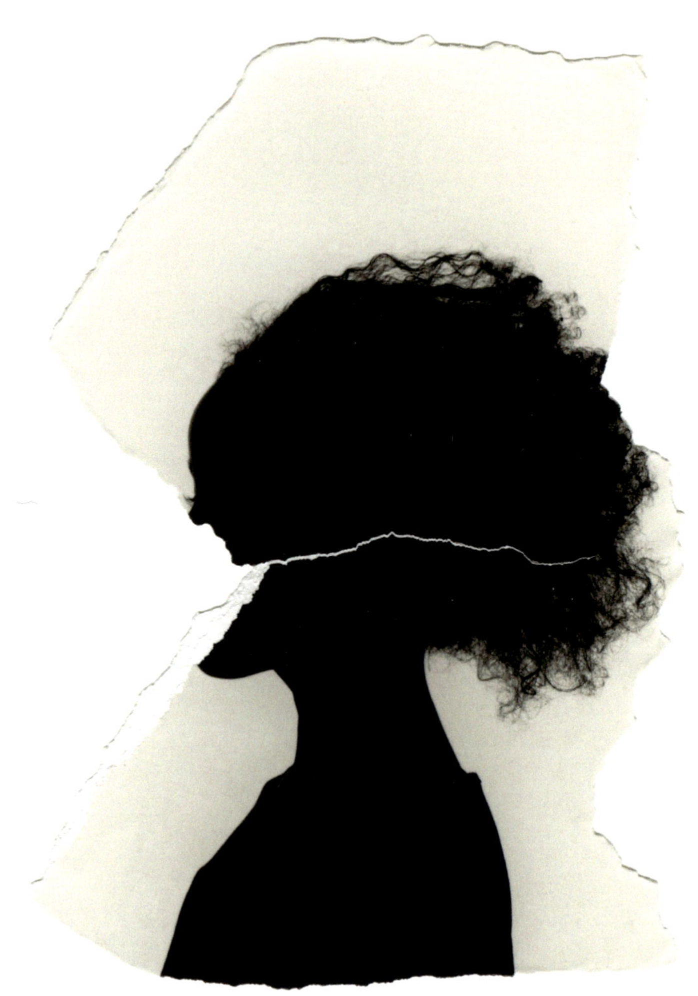

He knew, even if he could not make the explicit admission to himself, that the photos had become an alibi for his non-life. To take an action or decision, to seek to realize any desire or ambition, was unthinkable for as long as they came. He could not say why the child had become an ever more impassable obstacle to living. In the wordless face, he heard some warning or plea or command or siren call to stop just where he was, back riveted to the bottom stair, gaze to the photo.

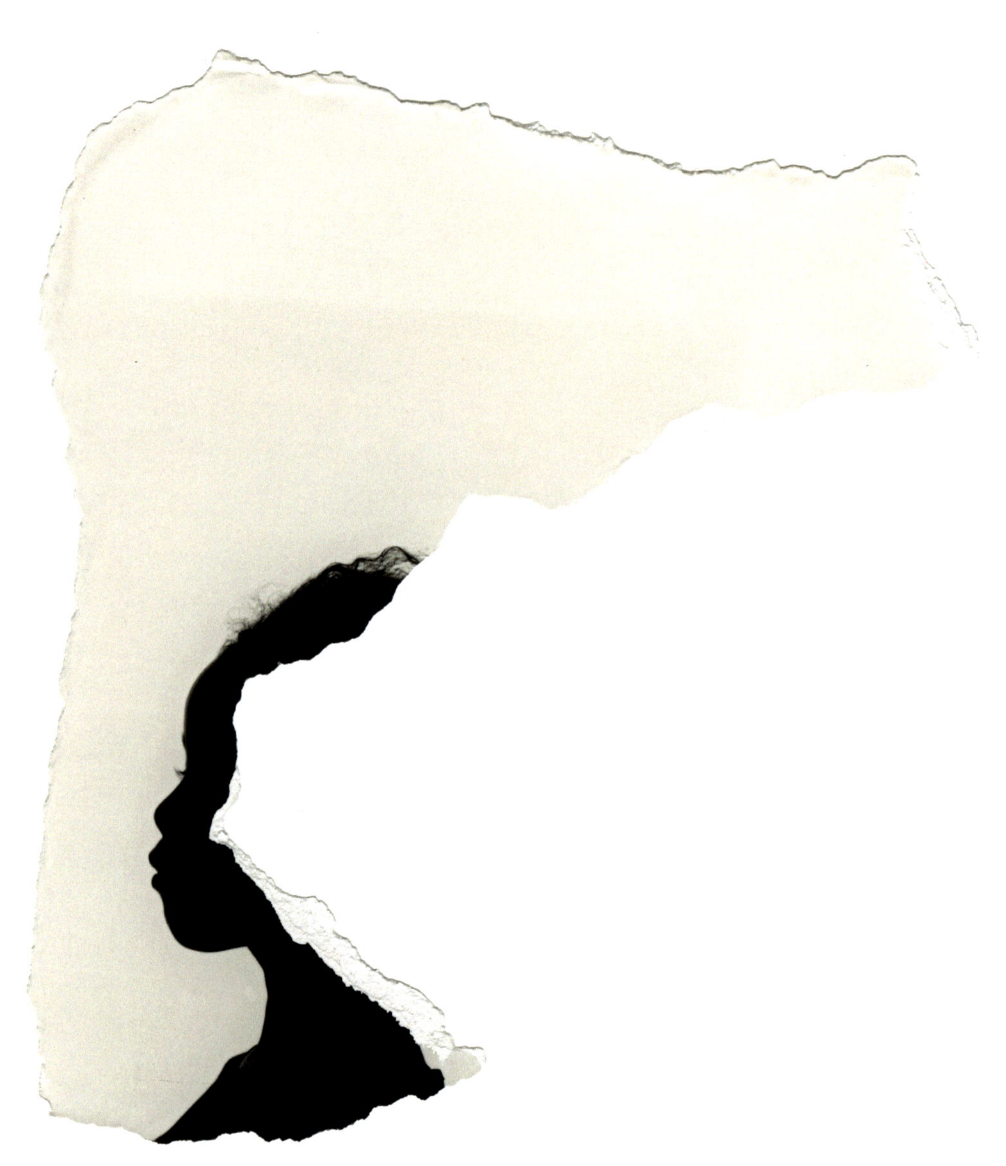

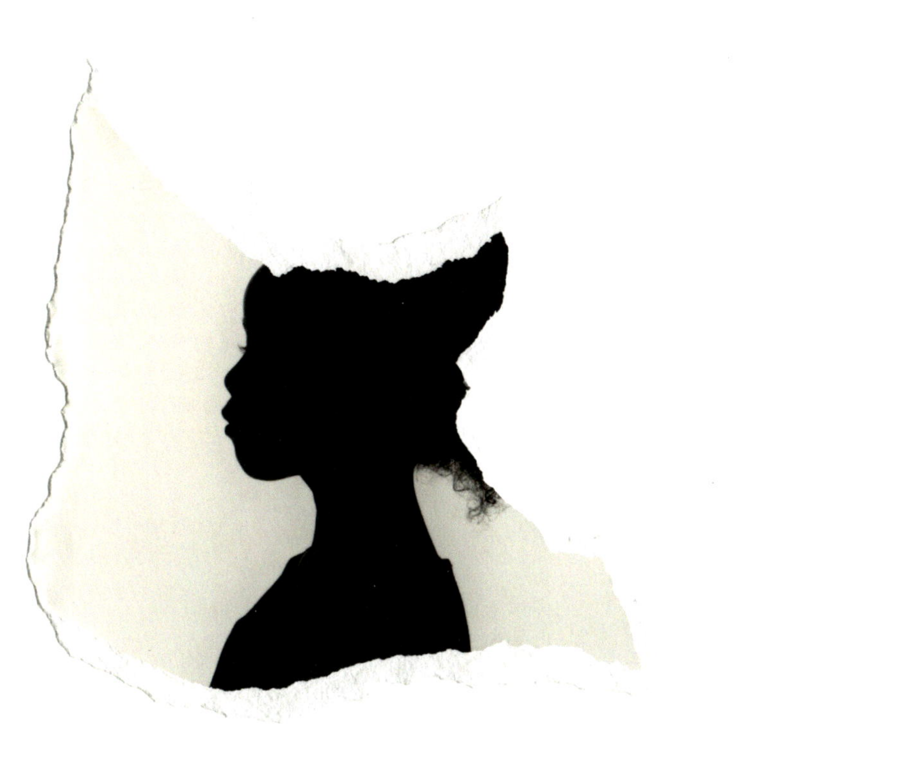

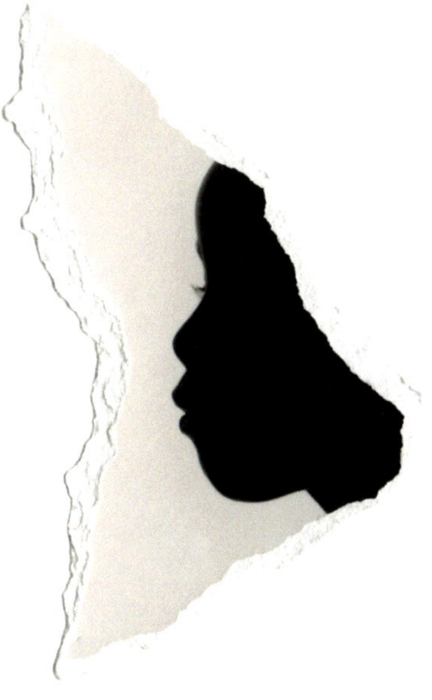

Yet as he gave way to this irresistible stasis, Wakeman felt something happening in him as though for the first time in his life, something cracking the frozen sea that had been his element for longer than he could recall. Scenes, suspended somewhere between memories and dreams, came to life in his mind and took possession of him.

In some small Mediterranean city, he sits alone in a playground sandpit, sluggish with late spring heat. As he stands, a curly-headed boy wearing a worn football shirt fills his field of vision. His eye becomes a pinhole camera, casting in darkness the world around him, everything but the angry head above the shirt, jerking in rhythm with the boy's righteous yelling. Already the space between them has collapsed, yet still the boy gets closer, until he's swallowed body and soul by his inexplicable rage, by his guttural vowels and plosive consonants, resounding with both mockery and plaintive reproach. Without understanding what he's done, he submits to it all.

He sprints down a grey suburban high street, feeling an electric joy pulse through his thighs, groin and scrawny chest, a joy that impels him impossibly far beyond his ordinary speed, his super-heroic mania transmitted through the flapping of the five-pound note held in his little fingers' claw grip as he anticipates the alchemy of exchanging it for something he wants.

It’s his own childhood that’s being sent to him.

In his *Natural History* of AD 77–9, Pliny the Elder famously ascribes the origin of painting to a young Corinthian maid 'who, being deeply in love with a young man about to depart on a long journey, traced the profile of his face, as thrown upon the wall by the light of the lamp'. Following his departure, her father fills out the outline with clay to create a relief.

A century later, Athenagoras' version of the story has the enamoured girl trace her beloved's outline while he sleeps. This state of sleep amplifies an ambiguity in the earlier version as to whether the tracing memorializes the living man she loves or his absence. Prone on the ground, withdrawn from the world in a state of inert silence, the sleeper is both here and elsewhere, a kind of harbinger of his own death. If sleep is already an absence, the image of sleep doubles that absence.

Love, loss and art converge in the shadow. Art, according to the legend of the Corinthian maid, begins with the discovery that every element of reality has its shadowy double. In the history of literature, the figure of the double – Poe's William Wilson, Stevenson's Mr Hyde – always presages the unravelling of the self, a repository of all his destructive, excessive and entropic impulses. Doubling is not simply a discrete theme of art, but its very substance. Words and images conjure an elusive, insubstantial double of the external world. '*Ceci n'est pas une pipe*' means that a sentence or picture is always an abstraction and emptying of that which it describes or depicts, a 'murder', as Maurice Blanchot has it, of the thing itself.

Art is the harnessing of this power to at once reproduce reality and rob it of its substance. In his essay 'Reality and Its Shadow', Emmanuel Lévinas, philosopher of the primacy of ethics, seems both fascinated and troubled by the existence of this parallel world of shadows we call art. The image, he points out, 'disincarnates' reality: 'A represented object, by the simple fact of becoming an image, is converted into a non-object.' Where objects in reality are subject to change and development, objects in an artwork are immobilized, petrified, 'shut up [like] prisoners', condemned to the self-same existence at every moment.

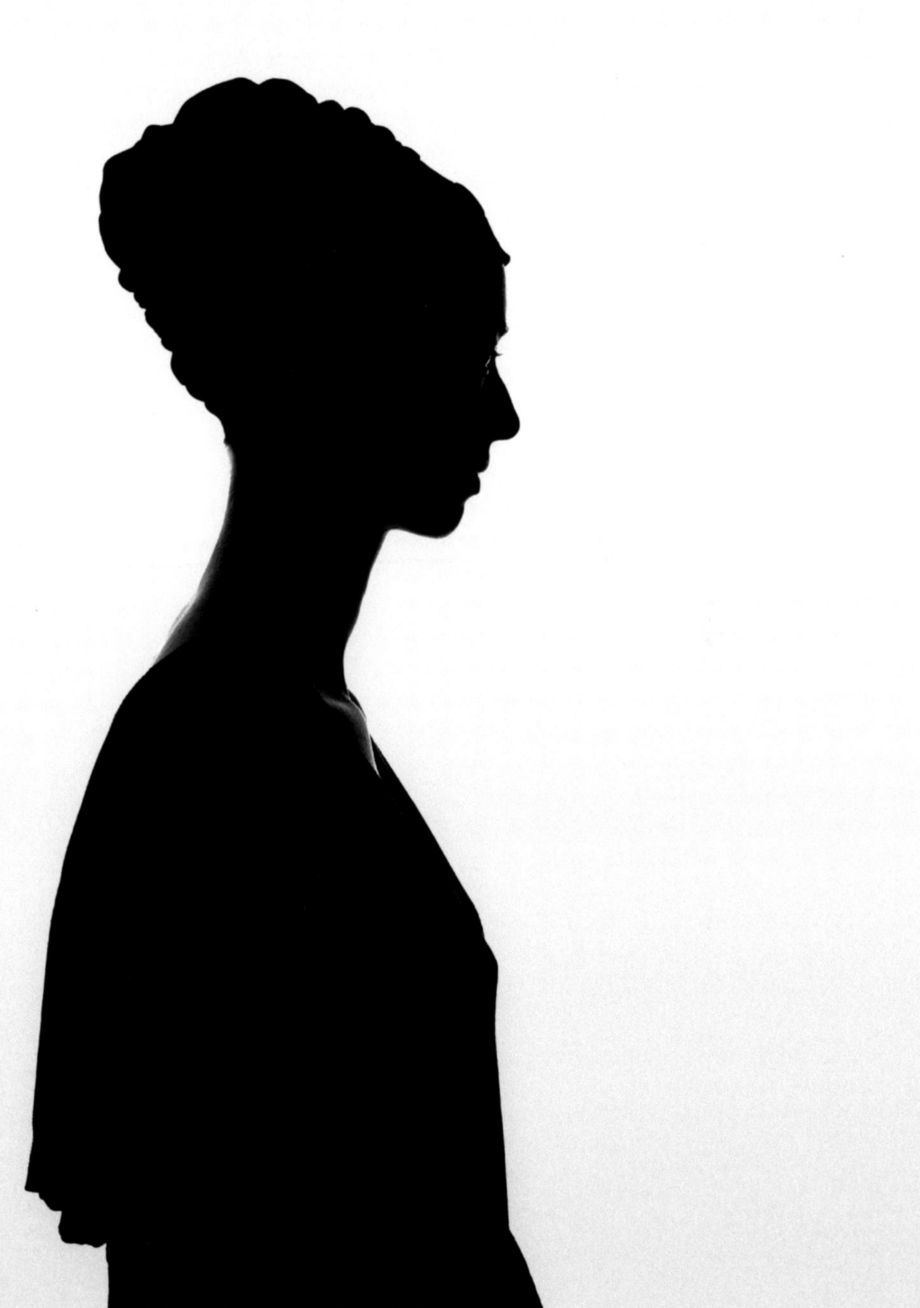

Even the characters in a novel, for all their apparent freedom, are consigned to the permanent repetition of the same lives. Insofar as they are immune to change, Lévinas suggests, the beings conjured by an artwork are essentially irresponsible. And this irresponsibility spreads to all of us on whom artworks cast their spell. To lose oneself in art is to forsake living reality and its demands for the evasive pleasures of a shadowy unreality.

There is thus a fundamental affinity between art and loss, embodied in the act of the Maid of Corinth. The young woman's invention of painting coincides with her lover's abandonment. At the point of his departure, she displaces her investment in him to his shadow, as though choosing his eternally petrified double over his mortal, fleshly reality. It is tempting to wonder quite who is leaving whom – while the lover leaves her for another region of the same world, the Maid embraces another world altogether.

This other world calls to mind a clinical case, recounted by D. W. Winnicott in his celebrated essay on 'transitional objects', of a woman who had been evacuated at age eleven, during the war, and had wiped out her childhood and parents from her memory as a result. She is able to maintain her parents only in the negative – that is, by managing never to give a name to her temporary carers. For this patient, Winnicott remarks, 'the only real thing is the gap; that is to say, the death or the absence or the amnesia … The amnesia is real, whereas what is forgotten has lost its reality.'

This orientation to the 'gap' is consummated in the patient's transferences to a previous analyst and to Winnicott, of whom she comments: 'The negative of him is more real than the positive of you.' It is difficult to think of a more perfectly compressed formulation of the Corinthian maid's displacement of her love from the young man to his shadow.

It is this preference for the negative rather than the substance of reality, observes Blanchot, that so often renders writers and artists suspect to men and women of action. A writer may dedicate himself to a cause, and for a while even persuade the proponents of that cause that he is on their side. But writers so

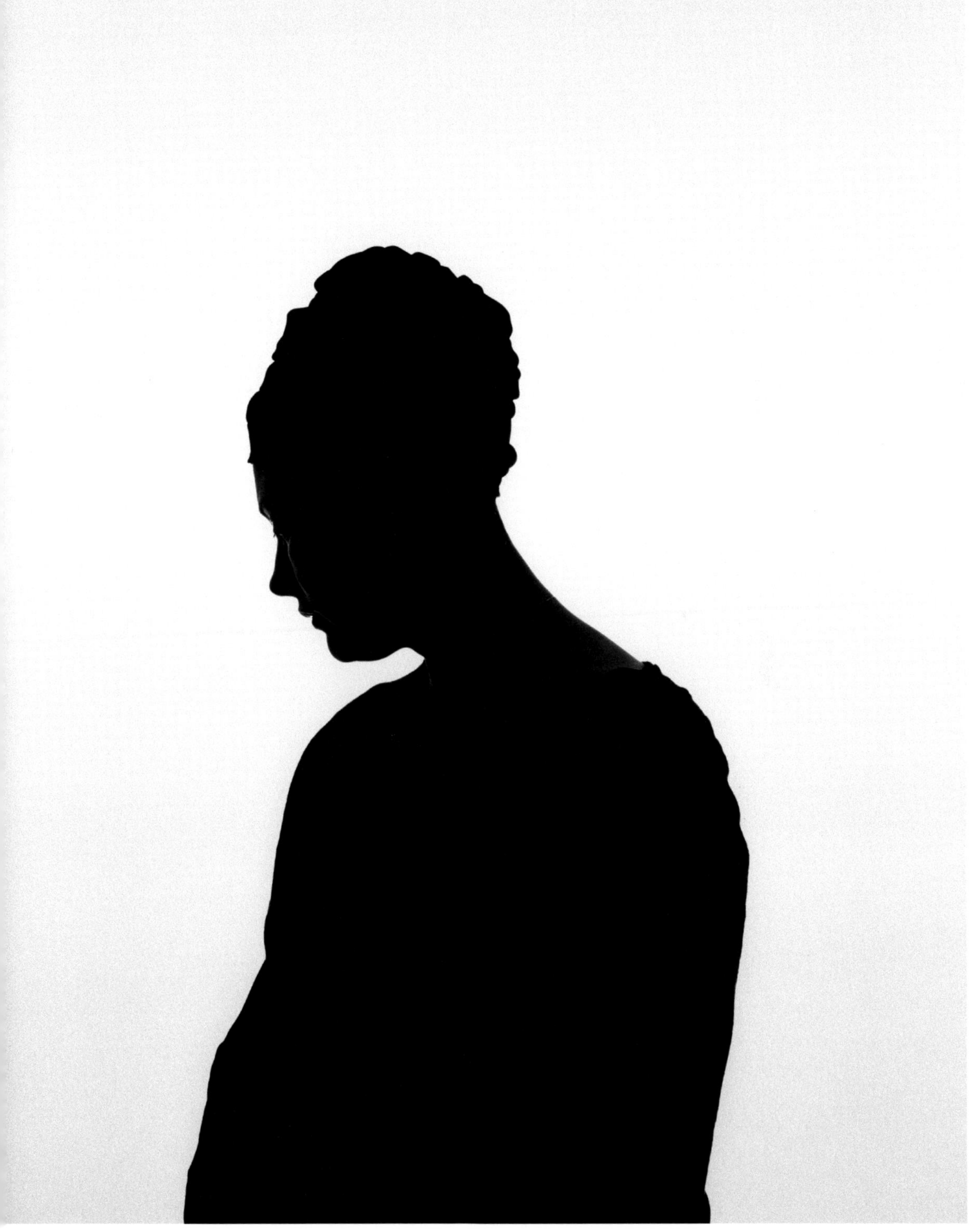

often end up being shunned, imprisoned or killed by the agents of revolution or reaction because the latter begin to discern, not without justification, that a devotion to art is a profound enemy of devotion to action.

The artist is punished, we might say, for pledging himself to the negative of life, to a shadowy imposter pretending to life. The modern totalitarian persecution of art belongs to the lineage of the Platonic philosopher-king. And in fact, just here the spectre of mourning surfaces again, for Socrates' prime example of the moral duplicity of art is precisely the poetic or dramatic representation of grief. Homer and the tragedians, observes Socrates, make a pleasurable spectacle of the torments of grief. Theatrical grief is shameless, 'womanish'. It holds up as an object of admiration the kind of 'uninhibited indulgence' that would disgust us in ordinary life. It brazenly exposes, not only in the performer but in the spectators, the extremities of feeling that reason compels us to control. It overwhelms the light with darkness, flooding our ears and minds with the senseless wailing that overwhelms all restraint and all rationality.

Grief, in other words, is a plunge into obscurity. Eight centuries later, Augustine, recalling the death of the beloved friend of his youth, writes: 'I carried my lacerated and bloody soul when it was unwilling to be carried by me. I found no place where I could put it down.... Everything was an object of horror, even light itself.' Mourning is the enemy of light, a kind of proclamation of the total sovereignty of darkness and the willing surrender of the soul to the fog of incomprehension. Socrates' charge against art is that it aggravates this fog instead of seeking to clear it away.

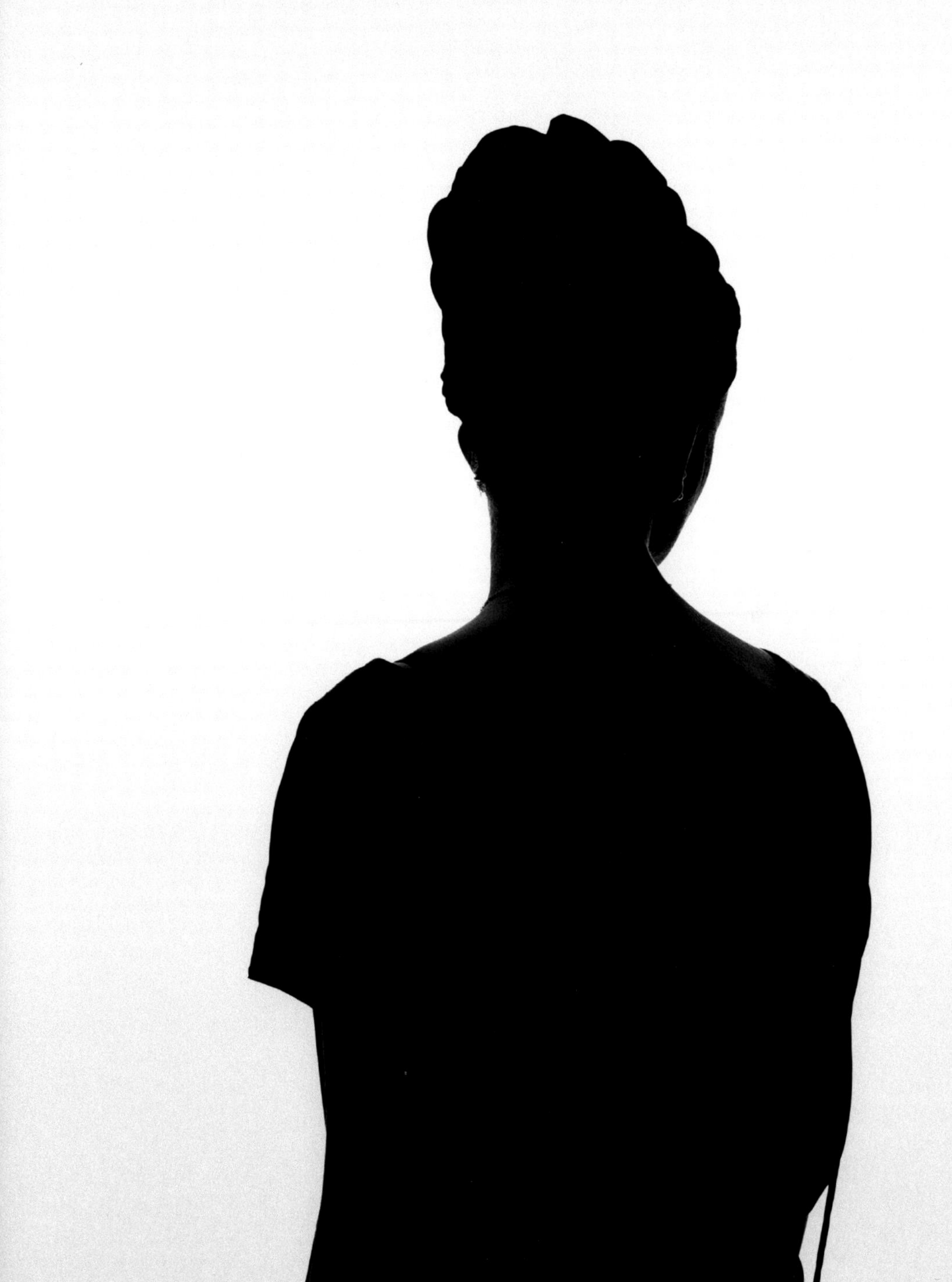

But does he want it?

Slumped

again

on the

bottom

stair,

the question comes to him, along with the observation, pitched somewhere between gratitude and resentment, that he never asked for it. Was it grace or damnation that the boy's face was visiting upon him?

He imagined sealing up his mailbox with duct tape, plugging up the gap between the front door and floor, blocking off all possible points of communication between his home and the outside world, building a fortress against all contact. He would redirect all mail to a locked box somewhere where it would remain uncollected and unread.

He would be restored to his unagitated adult life, to its predictably low and even flow, the ghost children pressing in on him from within and without banished to oblivion. He would rise steadily in the bank, earning back and then increasing his diminished credit, till this brief period of slackness would be dismissed as an aberration, about which it would be wiser and more discreet to remain silent. He would once again nurture his carefully circumscribed collegial friendships, perhaps even give himself over once in a while to odd episodes of efficient rutting and puttering romance.

Yes, with the boy's face exiled from his days, he could once again steer a clear path through the world, free of obstacles, detours, diversions. All choices, all wishes from this point on, would be directed towards this same freedom from surprise, from the burden of an eventful life.

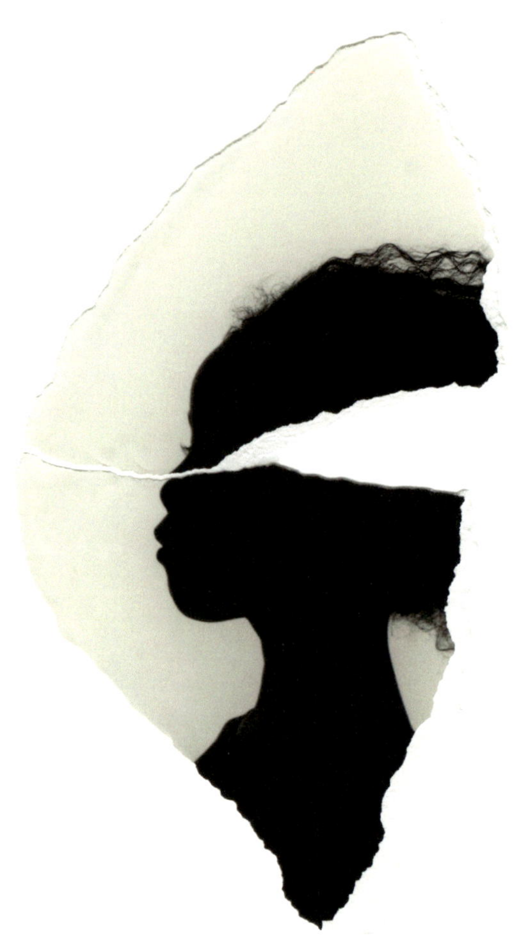

But the photos did not cease to come, nor did he redirect or burn them or throw them out with the junk mail. He remained riveted to the foot of the stairs, ravaged by the abundance of life and defiance streaming out of this young face, wanting to ask it what it wanted, to elicit the answer that must be hidden in or behind it.

His slouching vigils ate into ever greater portions of the day. There had been no explicit decision to renounce life beyond the front door, only an incremental daily increase, each very small, in his resistance to raising himself, until he realized that whole hours, then mornings, then days had passed.

If art sides with darkness and scientific knowledge with light, where does Freud place himself? His own explicit statements are unambiguous. Imaginative writers, he says in more than one place, are a primary source of access to the unconscious on account of their profound intimacy with it, their capacity to maintain contact with the deepest layers of fantasy life. But they suffer the disadvantage of having to deliver pleasure to their readers, such that they can never take sufficient distance from psychic life to examine it dispassionately. The writer's privilege and handicap is that he speaks out of the obscurity of his unconscious, whereas the man of science (with whom Freud is so fully identified) brings to the unconscious the clarifying light of his disinterested gaze.

This is how it is that Freud so often seems to 'explain' works of art, to resolve their enigmas, to shine the light of knowledge into their shadowy contents. Art assumes the essentially instrumental value of bringing to life the clinical and theoretical insights of psychoanalysis.

But the Freudian text always says more than it knows. Take his 1907 essay on Wilhelm Jensen's *Gradiva*, ostensibly a seamless exposition of the theories of repression and the unconscious by means of a reading of 'dreams and delusions' as they are played out in Jensen's light-hearted romance, focusing on the young scholar Norbert Hanold's delusional delirium during his visit to Pompeii. His mania centres on his conviction that the young woman he repeatedly sees around the ruins is Gradiva, the figure depicted on one of the city's frescos, come to life. The delusion is cemented by a dream, in which Hanold finds himself in Pompeii on the day of its destruction, somehow able to experience its horrors without danger. When he sees Gradiva stepping through the streets, he gives a warning cry, 'whereupon she turned her face towards him for a moment. But she proceeded on her way without paying any attention to him, lay down on the steps of the Temple of Apollo, and was buried in the rain of ashes after her face had lost its colour, as though it were turning into white marble, until it had become just like a piece of sculpture.'

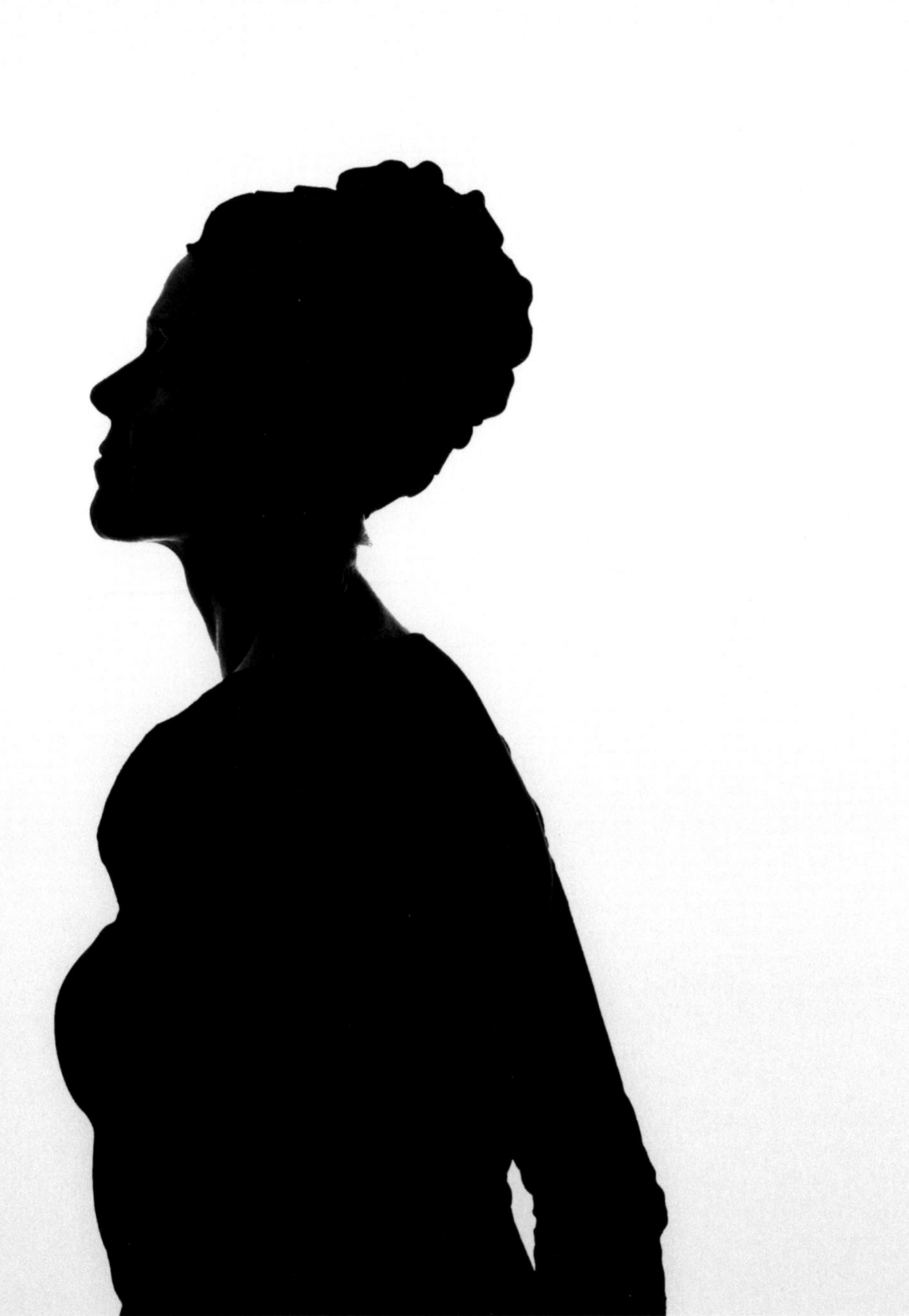

For Freud, this transformation of living flesh into dead stone illustrates acutely the mechanism of repression. The woman Hanold sees is in fact his childhood sweetheart Zoë, the memory of whom he has repressed. The erotic longing stirred up by the living Zoë (the name means 'life' in Greek), undergoes reversal in Hanold's dreams and delusions, manifesting itself as 'the destruction of Pompeii and the loss of Gradiva'. But in turning Hanold's passion for Zoë / Life to stone – by *petrifying* it – he goes beyond mere repression and into something like Lévinas's region of radical immobility. Zoë's live flesh is absorbed into the inanimacy of marble; reality is taken over by its shadow.

Six years later, Freud's beautiful paper 'The Theme of the Three Caskets' deepens the relationships between love, death and art. Two scenes from Shakespeare – the casket scene of *The Merchant of Venice* and the opening scene of *King Lear* – are invoked to illustrate the motif of the hero's 'choice between three' – caskets in the former, daughters in the latter. Cross-referencing Bassanio's choice of the lead casket in *The Merchant of Venice*, after his rivals have selected the gold and silver options, and thereby winning the coveted Portia's hand in marriage, to various folkloric and fairy-tale sources, Freud finds a recurring motif of lead as 'the bringer of fortune'. The essential virtue of lead, moreover, is intimately allied to its dumbness, hinting at a likeness between Bassanio's third casket and Cordelia, the third daughter of Lear: 'Lead is dumb – in fact like Cordelia, who "loves and is silent".'

Freud thus unearths a universal narrative pattern in which desire gravitates towards 'concealment and dumbness', silence and death. Art, the two papers whisper, hint at a relation between life and death defined not by opposition but by uncanny intimacy. As they avowedly choose life and love, Bassanio and Lear are inexorably caught in the lure of silence, concealment and death. This ruse is of art itself: for all that artworks can say so much, their ultimate destiny is to the muteness of stone and lead.

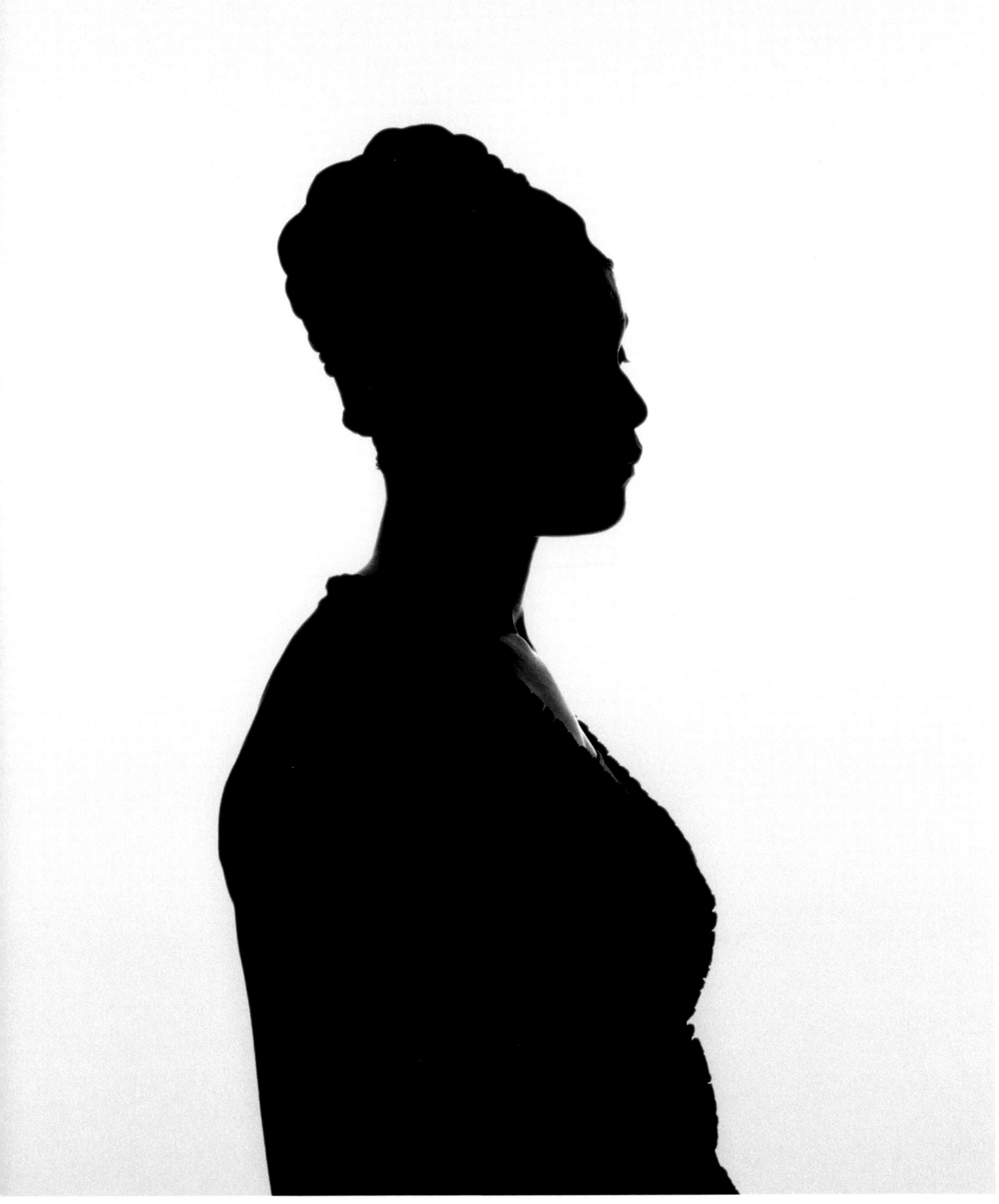

The waves of discomfort that swept through his gut when the telephone first rang soon abated, until he could register it with the same indifference as the rubbish truck's low hum or next door's yapping schnauzer. Somewhere, he knew, baffled, anxious and angry messages were accumulating on voicemail, email, text. He preferred to imagine rather than read or listen to them, responding to their contents with the quizzical curiosity you would reserve for someone else's messages, which in a way is what they were. His mind's eye scanned a sequence of electronic appeals from a series of line managers, polite at first, then jocose, concerned, angry and desperate in turn.

Letters arrive each day, piling unopened on the mat. He spies a small magnolia envelope and imagines himself removing the single sheet of notepaper, on which he finds an unconvincingly breezy greeting from a woman he'd accompanied to dinner weeks ago, perhaps to bed, he couldn't remember. She wondered where he'd disappeared to, exclamation mark.

The right-hand corners of the envelopes are stamped 'Urgent' with increasing frequency. The most recent is windowed, brilliant white, and brings to mind unbidden the boyhood image of a console table piled with letters addressed to everyone but him. He pictures the bank's solemn headed paper, the satisfyingly compact rectangles of dark black type informing him of the imminent termination of his contract following his unexplained absence of the last four weeks.

In his hand,
he holds the
one message
that still
reaches him.

The origin of art, the legend of the Corinthian girl tells us, is the trace of a shadow. Her departing lover takes his shadow when he leaves; only her tracing of it remains. Works of art are a means of holding on to the objects that slip from our grasp.

In this regard at least, they resemble the melancholic as described by Freud, on whom 'the shadow of the object' famously falls. Unable to give him up for dead, the melancholic instead identifies herself with the one she has lost, takes him into herself and lives cast in his shadow. Though apparently occupying the same world as us, she speaks and acts as though she were somewhere else, in some fold inhabited by the dead and woven imperceptibly into the space-time of the living. So much of her inner life has been siphoned off into that elsewhere that what remains in this one seems thin, superficial even, as though her self is being played by a mediocre actor.

Looking at Bettina von Zwehl's *Laments*, in the first instance at least, is not unlike falling headlong into that fold. Immersed in shadow, faces turned away or concealed, the women seem intensely aware of soliciting the gaze that they evade. At the very moment that they have withdrawn from shared space, slipped into a private region where they cannot be reached, they are caught in the consciousness of being looked at, appearing to merge into their art-historical allusions.

But those allusions – to Regency miniatures and painted silhouettes – do not confer easy legibility on these figures. On the contrary, they are invoked only to plunge the women, and the gaze that contemplates them, into a region of invisibility. The invisible here is not, as in the traditional silhouette, the other of the visible, so much as its intimate companion. Physiognomy, comportment, feelings are all revealed not through light but through darkness; shadows give us access to elements of the self that no light could reach.
No doubt the flowing contours of the sculpted head, exposed neck and curved bust, caressed by a nocturnal light that seems to emanate imperceptibly from within, amplify the erotic charge of these pictures. But this charge feels to me

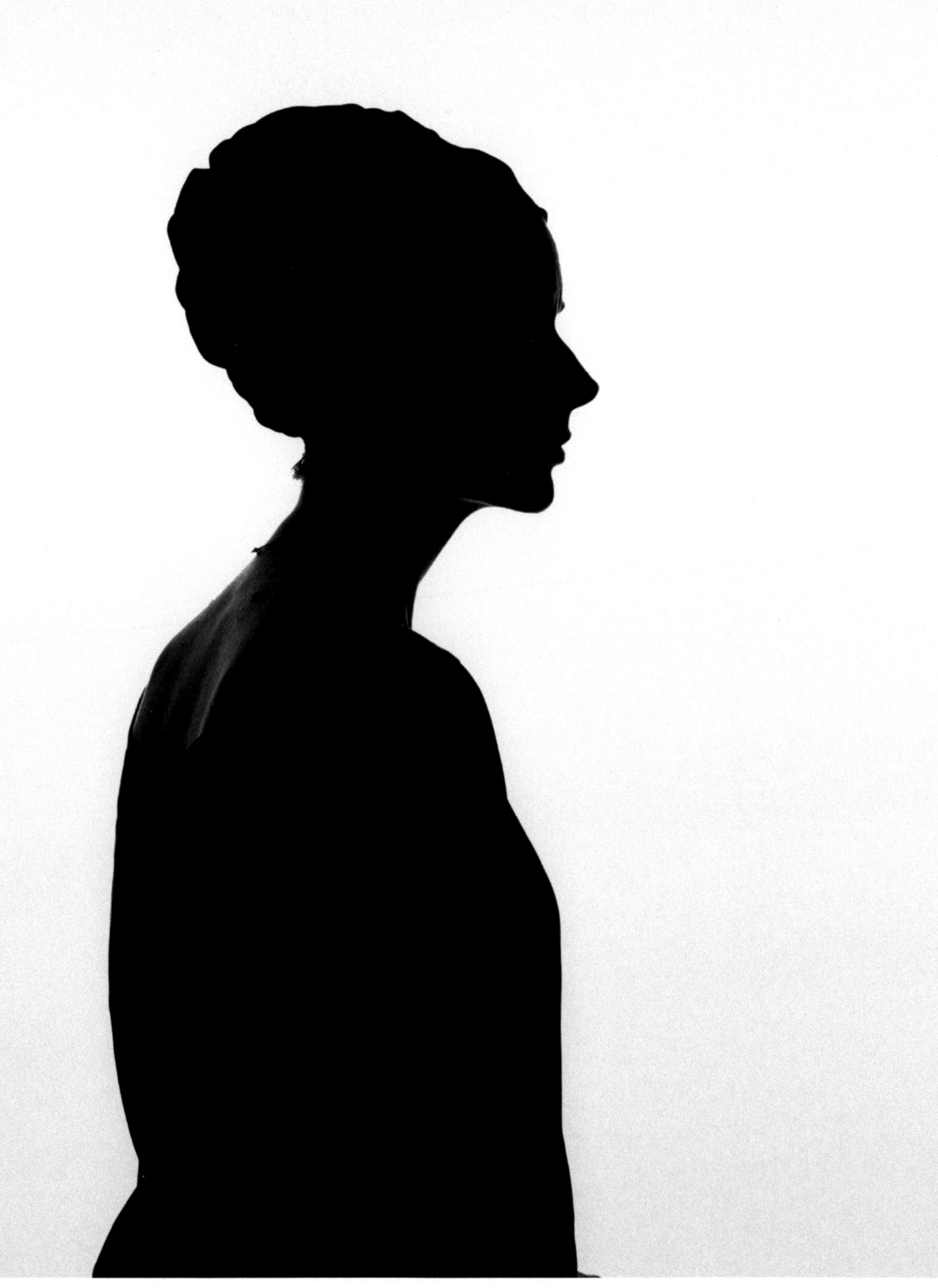

to have more to do with the desire they arouse and even, impossibly, gratify – to see the other not in her presence but in her absence.

The formulation of Winnicott's patient – 'The negative of him is more real than the positive of you' – finds its startling realization in these images. You might have expected the darkness to drain the blood from these figures, to render them abstract, thin, insubstantial. Instead it endows them with a fleshly reality more palpable and more present than any flashgun or ceiling light could hope to achieve.

These *Laments* are exposures, to be sure. They reveal the human as a lamenting being, destined to live with loss and absence. Following the Corinthian maid's example, they expose both the figures in the photographs and we who contemplate them to this destiny, reminding us, in silent defiance of our culture's tyrannizing transparency, that the truest exposure keeps us hidden.

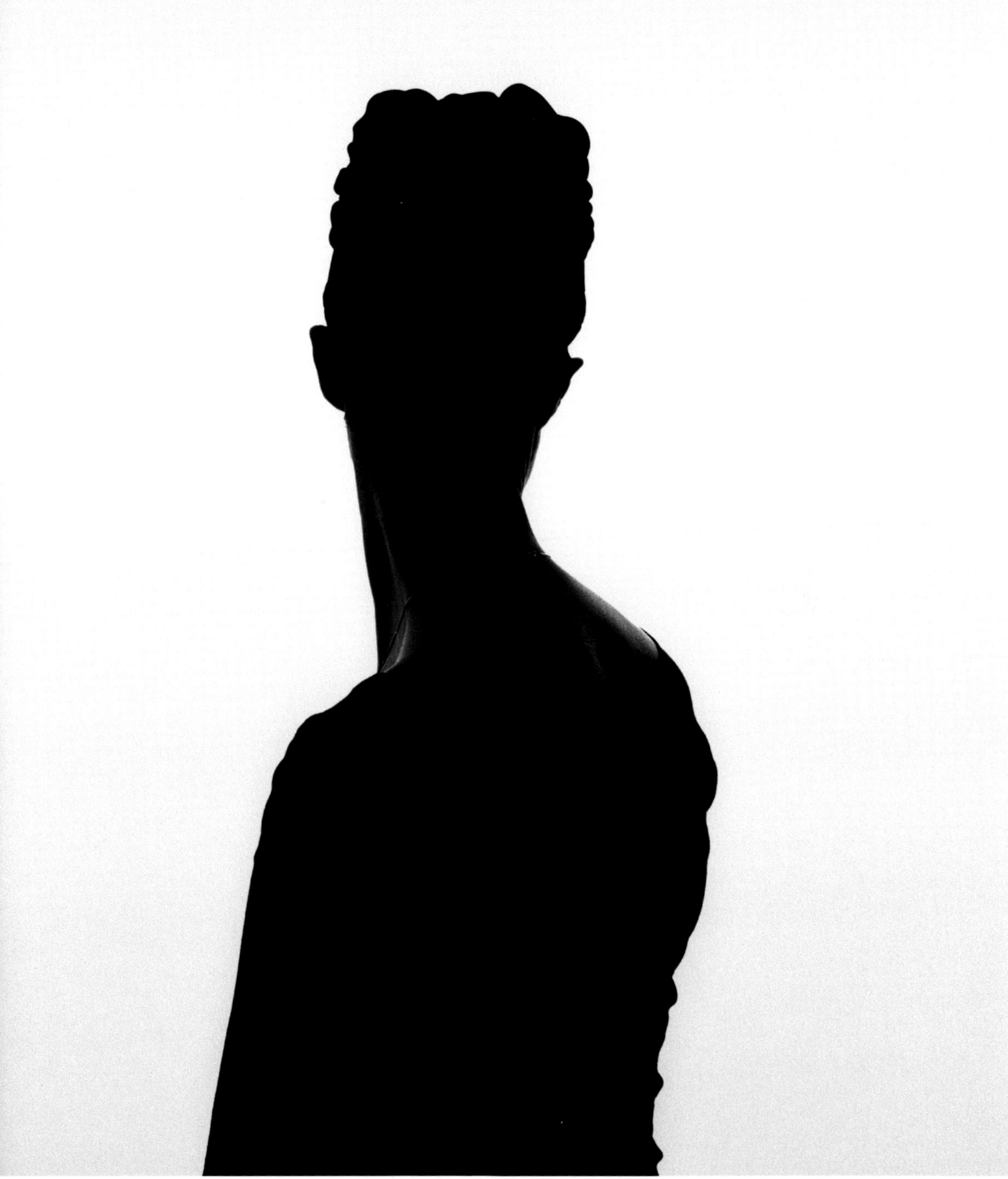

Space inexorably contracted around him. He placed a low table at his feet, under which he made a makeshift and renewable larder of crackers, tinned fish, boiled sweets, from which, once or twice a day, he satisfied the listless demands of his stomach. He walked to the toilet, the washbasin, the bed, the kitchen cupboards, satellites of the new centre of his life, those inches between the photo in his hand and the eyes that beheld it.

Strange that the more his life reduced itself to its barest elements, the more it bubbled up within him. It surprised him to discover it wasn't his own tomb he'd been making, that he didn't want to sink into a quiet death. Even as his joints ached and strained from the hours and days of rigid immobility, his inner ear attuned itself ever more intimately to the rise and fall of his breath, the unbroken rhythm of his heart, the flow of his blood.

Leaning over the low table, every twitch and flicker of his limbs, eyes and nose, every itch of his skin and groin, was a journey more venturesome than any he'd taken across the world.

The envelopes were a collapsed mountain, the most recent arrivals scattered closest to him, streaked in red. Breaking the unwritten proscription on where he could go, he walked to the study and lifted the phone's receiver to hear only the noisy void of his inner ear.

The house went dark,

then cold.

He tore the boy's head, shadowy or floodlit, in grainy close-up or fuzzy long-shot, from out of its surrounds, scattering the fragments across the table.

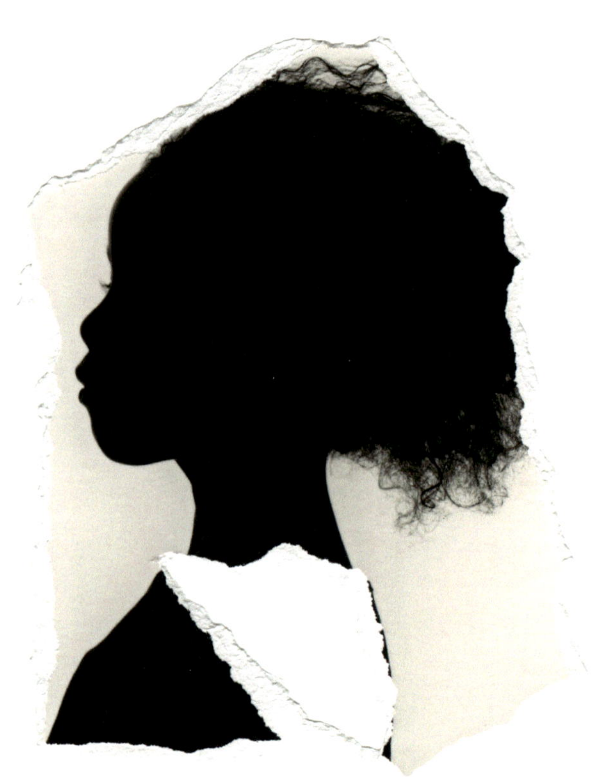

In the twilit hall, a shaft of fast-fading light cast over the contours of the face, he felt the complementary fading of his own self. He plunged himself again into the child's averted gaze for one last time before night overtook it.

He hoisted himself up in the darkness and, dissolving in the pain, slowly stretched his whole body, somehow still young, towards the

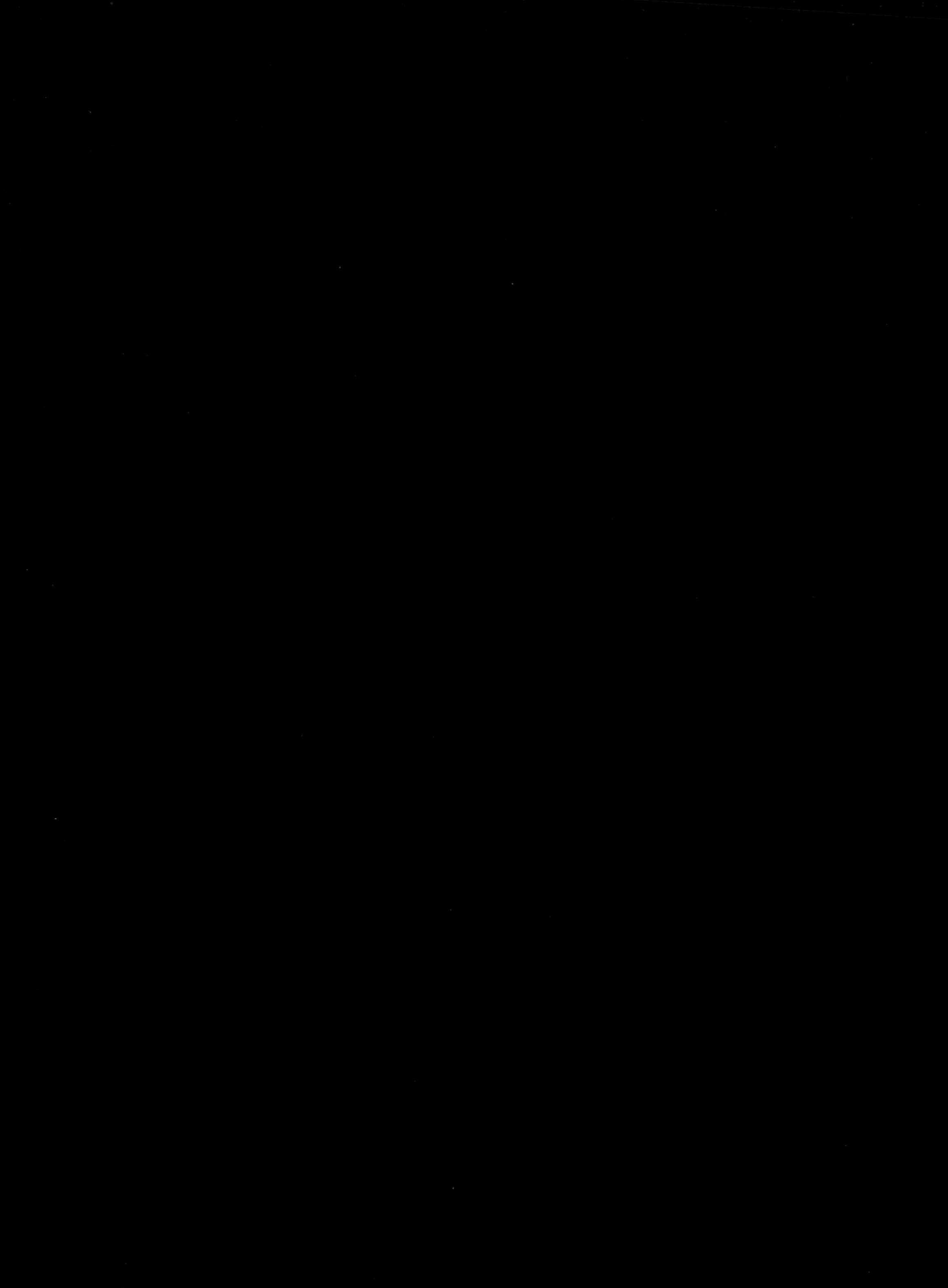

ceiling.

PUBLISHER'S NOTE

This volume brings together two sets of images and two pieces of writing to create a unique hybrid work of art and letters. Bettina von Zwehl produced *Laments*, her series of fifteen silhouette portraits of women in near darkness, following a residency at the Freud Museum in London in 2013/14. Inspired by Anna Freud's passionate letters with women friends, they are an expression of the female bonds in the artist's own life after the sudden death of a close friend.

She also made *The Sessions*, fifty fragments of a single photo of a young girl, in response to her study of the life and legacy of Anna Freud, as well as her own experience of psychoanalysis. The title refers to the patient's fifty-minute session with the analyst, the artist's sessions with the child, and her many sessions in the darkroom as she sought the essence of both image and subject. She made each piece by first tearing the photographic paper and then exposing the chosen negative onto it. By breaking down one moment repeatedly and obsessively in this way, infinite possibilities, failures and associations are opened up. At the same time, the torn fragments form an archive of scraps and 'mistakes' that echoes the seemingly 'unimportant' material stored in the mind of the analysand – material that has the potential to illuminate the patient's deepest issues.

Josh Cohen's short story 'The Arrivals' was in turn written as a response to these fragments, while also evoking various ideas and scenes he had himself encountered in analysis. His parallel essay, 'Invitation to Frequent the Shadows', is a critical reflection on light and shadow, art and artifice, and truth and lies prompted by his reading of the *Laments* portraits, and it continues his ongoing investigations into darkness, privacy and the hidden self.

Each series of photographs and text can be read separately, but it is through the combination and interplay of word and image that a new narrative emerges and an additional layer of meaning appears in the gaps, folds and blurred edges between the two. The result is a powerful and moving meditation on the themes of light and dark, love and loss, life and death.

Bettina von Zwehl is an artist living and working in London.

Josh Cohen is a psychoanalyst and writer and teaches at Goldsmiths, University of London.

The artist would like to thank Helene Klausner-Huth for her generous support of this publication

First published in the United Kingdom in 2016 by
Art Books Publishing Ltd

Art Books Publishing Ltd
77 Oriel Road
London E9 5SG
T: +44 (0)20 8533 5835
info@artbookspublishing.co.uk
www.artbookspublishing.co.uk

British Library Cataloguing-in-Publication Data
A catalogue record for this book is available from the British Library

ISBN 978-1-908970-27-5

Designed by Art/Books
Repro: JK Morris Production AB, Värnamo
Printed and bound in Latvia by Livonia

Distributed outside North America by
Thames & Hudson
181a High Holborn
London WC1V 7QX
United Kingdom
T: +44 (0)20 7845 5000
F: +44 (0)20 7845 5055
sales@thameshudson.co.uk

Available in North America through
ARTBOOK | D.A.P.
155 Sixth Avenue, 2nd Floor,
New York, N.Y. 10013
www.artbook.com